Editors of
Guideposts

TIME OUT
IN TOUGH TIMES

*Two-Minute Quiet Times
to Soothe the Spirit*

MJF BOOKS
New York

Published by MJF Books
Fine Communications
322 Eighth Avenue
New York, NY 10001

Time Out in Tough Times
LC Control Number: 2012930201
ISBN-13: 978-1-60671-126-2
ISBN-10: 1-60671-126-1

Acknowledgments:
Every attempt has been made to credit the sources of copyrighted material used in this book.
If any such acknowledgment has been inadvertently omitted or miscredited, receipt of such
information would be appreciated.

All Scripture quotations, unless otherwise noted, are taken from *The King James Version of the Bible.*

Scripture quotations marked (NIV) are taken from *The Holy Bible, New International Version.* Copyright
© 1973, 1978, 1984 International Bible Society. Used by permission of Zondervan Bible Publishers.

Scripture quotations marked (NKJV) are taken from *The Holy Bible, New King James Version.*
Copyright © 1997, 1990, 1985, 1983 by Thomas Nelson, Inc.

Scripture quotations marked (RSV) are taken from the *Revised Standard Version of the Bible.*
Copyright © 1946, 1952, 1971 by Division of Christian Education of the National
Council of Churches of Christ in the U.S.A. Used by permission.

Scripture quotations marked (TLB) are taken from *The Living Bible.*
Copyright © 1971 by Tyndale House Publishers, Wheaton, Illinois 60187. All rights reserved.

This edition is published by MJF Books in arrangement with Guideposts.

Printed in the United States of America.

MJF Books and the MJF colophon are trademarks of Fine Creative Media, Inc.

QF   10   9   8   7   6   5   4   3   2   1

CONTENTS

◄o►

INTRODUCTION

⟨○⟩

For all of us, there are times when we have to take a deep breath, step back from a stressful situation or a daunting challenge, and regain our composure. And when things are particularly difficult—when times are really tough—it may be harder for us to find the respite we need and the strength necessary to get past the problems and move on with our lives.

This book is designed to be your "spiritual first-aid kit"— whatever your need—to help you create a two-minute quiet time to compose your mind, give your worries over to God, Who watches over all of us, and resume your day with confidence and serenity. We've tried to make the volume easy to use. It's arranged by topic, with a table of contents, so that you can quickly find the entry you need. And we've provided each time-out with four easy steps:

- READ a Scripture verse to quiet and ground your spirit;

- REFLECT on a brief message from someone who understands what you're going through;

- PRAY to put your situation in God's hands;

- DO something simple that will help move you beyond your worries.

Whether you're facing illness, worrying about a loved one, struggling with your finances, facing problems at work, feeling stretched too thin or too far from God, it's our prayer that you will find sustenance and support in these pages. No matter how tough the times may be or how dark the moment may seem, they are held in God's hands. And in God's light, there is no shadow of darkness.

If you have a special need that you would like to see addressed in a future *Time-Out* book or if you would like prayer support, please write to *Time-Out*, Guideposts Books, 16 E. 34th Street, New York, NY 10016. We will be happy pray for you at our weekly Guideposts Prayer Fellowship.

—The Editors

WHEN A FRIEND FEELS INFERIOR TO OTHERS

READ: *If I must boast, I will boast of the things that show my weakness.*

—2 CORINTHIANS 11:30 (NIV)

REFLECT: Linda sat on my sofa and haltingly told me that she had always felt inferior to others. "Karen, you seem to have it all together," she said.

I tried to tell Linda that we're all quite human, and then I remembered a friend named Charlene.

I had been a newcomer in town; everyone I met seemed to dress so stylishly, their homes well-decorated. I had felt that I'd never fit in. One day Charlene invited me over. "Come upstairs," she said. She ushered me into her bedroom and showed me her unmade bed. "Now that you know I'm not perfect, we can be friends."

I turned toward Linda and said, "I want you to see something." I led her to the laundry room. The usual pile of dirty clothes was on the floor. By the time I opened the cabinet under the sink and a jumble of toys and crumpled paper fell out, Linda was smiling.

Linda used to think I was perfect. Now she just calls me her friend.

—KAREN BARBER

PRAY: *Lord, help _____ think only about Your perfection and seek to be like You.*

DO: Let your friends see your imperfections while introducing them to your perfect God.

WHEN A FRIEND
FEELS LIKE RETREATING

◄○►

READ: *For you, brethren, have been called to liberty; only do not use liberty as an opportunity for the flesh, but through love serve one another.*

—GALATIANS 5:13

REFLECT: Colorado drivers quickly learn the cardinal rule of winter driving: When sliding on ice, always steer into the direction of the skid. My instinctive reaction tells me to turn the wheel in the other direction. But I have to admit from experience that steering into the slide works.

I thought about this opposite solution the other day when I was feeling sad and discouraged. My instinctive reaction was to retreat within the protective solitude of my home. That's what I was doing when a friend phoned and asked me to fill in for her at the volunteer desk at the high school. It was the exact opposite of what I felt like doing, but for some reason I said, "Okay."

Several hours later I was driving home in a totally turned-around mood. Doing something for someone else was the very opposite of what I felt like doing, but it steered me out of my bad mood.

—CAROL KUYKENDALL

PRAY: *Lord Jesus, if anyone ever did the opposite of what he felt like doing, it's You when you went to the cross. Thank You for doing that for me.*

DO: Share the "opposite principle" with a discouraged friend.

WHEN A FRIEND
HAS FACED DANGER

---◄○►---

READ: *I will remember My covenant which is between Me and you and every living creature of all flesh.*

—GENESIS 9:15

REFLECT: My journalist friend Jan was on assignment in Afghanistan. She was traveling one night with a group of Afghans when their tiny convoy was attacked by helicopters strafing the road. They sped to the nearest village. When night fell, they made their way on foot to the base camp.

Back in the United States, Jan told me her story. "You know how nonreligious I am," she said. "Well, during the four hours it took us to reach the base that night, a song I sang as a little girl kept going through my mind, 'Do, Lord, oh, do, Lord, oh, do remember me....'"

"It looks as if He did remember you," I said.

She didn't answer right away; then she said, almost shyly, "I haven't been to church in years. Would you go with me this Sunday? I want to tell Him thank You for remembering me."

—SAMANTHA MCGARRITY

PRAY: *Your love is amazing, Father—remembering my friend _____ when he/she has chosen to forget You for so many years.*

DO: Ask God to remember other friends who have forgotten Him.

WHEN A FRIEND HAS MULTIPLE PROBLEMS

◄◦►

READ: *Have you comprehended the breadth of the earth? Tell Me, if you know all this.*

—JOB 38:18

REFLECT: Near Tucson, Arizona, stands an expensive experiment that didn't work. The Biosphere 2, a multistory bubble with sixty-five hundred windows, cost millions of dollars. It was painstakingly designed with rain forest, ocean, tropic and desert environments to support life. One day, its builders hoped, it might be reconstructed on Mars as a base for manned exploration. But their hope was unfulfilled. Scientists struggled to fix the Biosphere's oxygen-carbon dioxide imbalances, discovered that insects were essential, battled the premature dying of plants and animals and finally gave up.

One small discovery, however, struck me as profound: The cottonwood trees began falling over as they grew tall; they had to be propped up. Why? Because the scientists had not included wind in their world, and wind was necessary for cottonwoods to develop strong root structures.

Confusion, disappointment and death enter my life no matter how hard I try to avoid them. But, as with the cottonwoods, ill winds can help me develop strong roots and a deeper faith.

—MARJORIE PARKER

PRAY: *Prop me up, Lord, until my roots run deep.*

DO: Encourage your friend, through this story, that life's struggles are necessary.

WHEN A FRIEND HAS STRAYED FROM GOD

---◄◦►---

READ: *Because Christ also suffered for us, leaving us an example, that you should follow His steps. . . .*

—1 PETER 2:21

REFLECT: I'd taken my son John to southwest Nebraska to get his car. When we started home, the sun was down and fog had settled over the plains like a fat white hen roosting. As I fretted, John said, "It'll be all right, Mom. Just follow my taillights." When we pulled onto the road, I could feel the muscles at the back of my neck tighten. But as I focused on John's taillights, I began to relax. He had traveled this road many times and knew it well, even the bumpy detour. I knew I could trust him to get us safely home.

When there's a serious problem in my life and I can see no way out of the dilemma, I don't have to be able to see the road ahead at every turn. All I have to do is to keep my eyes on God's Son and let His light guide me. He knows the way. He'll lead me safely through the darkness.

—MARILYN MORGAN KING

PRAY: *Lord Jesus, my friend _____ has strayed so far from You he/she can't see Your light to follow. Would You help him/her find the way back to You?*

DO: Send a ray of Jesus' light out to your friend: A prayer, a Scripture, a word of encouragement about God's unconditional love.

WHEN A FRIEND HAS SUFFERED A LOSS

———————————◈———————————

READ: *Just as you share in our sufferings, so also you share in our comfort.*

—2 CORINTHIANS 1:7 (NIV)

REFLECT: Half past twelve, and little Wendy still hadn't come home for lunch. I called her friend's house and asked her mother to please send my daughter home. A few minutes later, Wendy came dragging dejectedly into the kitchen.

"What's wrong?" I asked. "Why didn't you come home at noon when you were supposed to?"

"Donna lost her birthday dollar," Wendy replied.

"Oh, I see. Did you stay longer to help her look for the money?"

"No, Mother, I just stayed to help her cry."

As I kissed Wendy's sweet cheek, the word *empathy* came to mind. More than "sympathy," which is looking down and pitying, empathy gets down and shares.

—ROSALYN HART FINCH

PRAY: *Jesus, You walked this earth as a man. You understand our losses because You experienced them Yourself. Please tell me how to comfort my friend.*

DO: Don't be afraid to let a friend see you cry for his/her loss.

WHEN A FRIEND IS DISCOURAGED

—◆◇◆—

READ: *Glorify the Lord with me; let us exalt his name together.*

—PSALM 34:3

REFLECT: Once a friend who was going through a divorce said, "I have nothing to be thankful for." I thought immediately of the privilege of living in God's incredibly beautiful world.

I was about to count her blessings for her—but, thank goodness, I stopped in time. We can never count another person's blessings. Besides, although I've never said, "I have nothing to be thankful for," there are times when I feel that way. So I decided that each morning I'd list three things for which I'm thankful, each one something I hadn't listed before. My list for today:

1. For the wonderful gift of loving and being loved.
2. For beautiful, white, billowing clouds in a blue sky.
3. For the gift of books—first of all the Bible—to be read and reread before I fall asleep at night.

And I know I'll never run out of new things to add to my list.

—ALETHA JANE LINDSTROM

PRAY: *I pray for _____ today, Lord. Give him/her blessings too numerous to overlook.*

DO: Write your friend to say you've added him/her to your list of blessings today.

WHEN A FRIEND IS DYING

<o>

READ: *For as in Adam all die, even so in Christ all shall be made alive.*

—1 CORINTHIANS 15:22

REFLECT: My good friend John was in the final stages of cancer. In a few moments I would leave South Carolina to return to Texas. I knew we would not see each other again this side of eternity.

Sitting by John's bedside, I suddenly thought of the silver cross I had worn around my neck for years, a reminder of my faith in difficult times.

I took off the cross and put it in John's hand. "This cross has been special to me for a long time," I said, "and I want you to have it. I can't be here with you in the days ahead. But maybe this cross can remind you of the faith we share that believes God can take death and change it into life." John started weeping. I did too.

A few weeks later, John died. But he left the cross for his wife to wear, a promise that they will meet again.

—SCOTT WALKER

PRAY: *I pray for _____ today, Lord. Prepare his/her heart to enter into eternity with You.*

DO: Find a symbol of your faith to share with a friend facing death.

WHEN A FRIEND IS EXPERIENCING "TURBULENCE"

<o>

READ: *You lift me up to the wind and cause me to ride on it. . . .*

—JOB 30:22

REFLECT: "This is the captain speaking. There's a lot of weather around Denver, so you might want to buckle up early as we try to land."

Whoa! What was that? Try to land? I dutifully fastened my seat belt. We were bouncing around like a Chihuahua on caffeine. Finally the runway came into sight. We were still all a jolt, but at least we were on the ground.

Wrong! The pilot aborted the landing and we went screaming skyward. After a few minutes of roller-coaster action, the pilot informed us that we were going to Colorado Springs. Some people applauded. No one complained about the abrupt delay.

How many times my life has met with rough weather, usually without the warning to buckle up. Birth, death, joy, sorrow—they pop up like a sudden thunderstorm. Sometimes you land. Sometimes you try to land, then take off again. Sometimes you end up in a completely different place, and there's nothing to do but call on the Almighty and ride it out.

—MARK COLLINS

PRAY: *Lord, the storms of life are tossing _____ about. Help him/her to remember that only You can say, "Peace, be still" (Mark 4:39).*

DO: Do a Bible study with your friend on the word *storm.*

WHEN A FRIEND IS FACING A DISAPPOINTMENT

READ: *Two are better than one . . . For if they fall, one will lift up his companion.*

—ECCLESIASTES 4:9–10

REFLECT: I liked the saying, "When life gives you lemons, make lemonade!" But after an experience our daughter had, I changed the words slightly.

Nikki was five and looking forward to the pet show her kindergarten teacher had announced. She couldn't wait to show off Putty, our black kitten, and admire her classmates' pets as well. Then life dumped a whole crateful of lemons on Nikki in the form of chicken pox. Grotesquely spotted and itchy, she felt too miserable to even enjoy staying home.

When she returned to school, I hoped she wouldn't be too dejected after hearing about the fun she had missed. Instead, she came home bursting with pride, carrying a shiny gold foil medallion with two blue construction paper ribbons dangling beneath. It said, "First Prize for Most Invisible Cat."

Do you know someone too discouraged today to see a bright side? I suggest that "When life gives your friends lemons, help them make lemonade!"

—B. J. CONNOR

PRAY: *Lord, show me what to do that will lift _____'s spirits.*

DO: Listen for an answer to your prayer and follow through with an idea that God gives you.

WHEN A FRIEND IS FACING A FINANCIAL CRISIS

―◄○►―

READ: *Yet man is born to trouble; as the sparks fly upward.*

—JOB 5:7

REFLECT: My friend and I were talking about the Great Depression, which both of us remember vividly.

"I couldn't get a job anywhere," he said. "No welfare, no unemployment insurance. I didn't know how I was going to live. I was scared!

"At that time the postal rate for letters went from two cents to three—a big jump! Then I had an idea. I took my last four dollars and bought a very second-hand bicycle. I went to all the merchants on Main Street and told them I would deliver their bills for a cent and a half apiece.

"Several of them took me on. I was able to earn about two dollars a day. With that you could buy a week's supply of groceries.

Yes, trouble can be painful. But if it makes you take action, you're bound to find your way through it. And maybe discover a new strength you didn't know you had.

—ARTHUR GORDON

PRAY: *Lord, You are my friend's provider. Provide for him/her now, through a job, unexpected finances, a fresh idea that will see him/her through this rough time.*

DO: Brainstorm with your friend on creative ways to make his/her talents productive.

WHEN A FRIEND IS FACING AN EMERGENCY

◄○►

READ: *Being in agony, He prayed more earnestly.*

—LUKE 22:44

REFLECT: The voice of my friend over the telephone asked for my prayers for her husband in the hospital. With a little sob in her throat she said, "I've never prayed so hard in all my life before."

I appreciated the fact that she had felt free to call upon me for prayer, and I joined her immediately. But I felt a twinge of guilt, asking myself why it is that we pray hardest only in the face of crisis.

This troubled me so much that, later on in my Bible reading, it was reassuring to come upon the passage that told me that even Jesus "prayed more earnestly" in his human agony of Gethsemane. It seems very human to neglect the power of prayer until we are brought face-to-face with some emergency. Surely our Heavenly Father understands.

—RUTH C. IKERMAN

PRAY: *Lord Jesus, thank You for the many ways You've modeled for us to pray.*

DO: Pray harder for a friend in crisis . . . and harder . . . and harder.

WHEN A FRIEND
IS FACING A TRIAL

◄○►

READ: *Do not harden your hearts . . . As in the day of trial in the wilderness.*

— PSALM 95:8

REFLECT: I hadn't talked to my friend Geoffrey in quite a while. Knowing that he was in the middle of an increasingly messy custody dispute, one Sunday after church I finally tracked him down.

"How are you?" I asked.

"Actually," he said, "I'm doing quite well. It's been hard, but my prayer life is amazingly strong. I stumbled onto a technique that has helped me enormously." I asked him what it was.

"Well, whenever I find myself getting really angry, I bring myself to the foot of the Cross and kneel there. And then I mentally bring my former wife to kneel at my side."

"Wow," I said, "that sounds really hard."

"Sometimes it takes a long time to let go enough to bring her there. But the way I look at it, if I can't kneel with someone in front of Jesus, my problems are much bigger than the problems I face in this world."

— JULiA ATTAWAY

PRAY: *Jesus, I kneel before You with* _____ *today.*

DO: Keep a small cross close to where you usually pray as a reminder to go there often.

WHEN A FRIEND
IS FRAZZLED BY LIFE

◄○►

READ: *How much more will your Father who is in heaven give good things to those who ask Him!*

—MATTHEW 7:11

REFLECT: A minister friend told me about a phone call he received one night. At one or two in the morning, he was awakened by a caller who was sobbing and rambling on in a way that made no sense. Trying to wake up, calm the caller and make sense of the problem, my friend became exasperated and said sternly, "Now settle down, get a grip on yourself and tell me your name."

In a moment came the startled reply, "But, Dad, it's me, Joel!"

Instantly my friend was wide awake, totally sympathetic, filled with love and compassion, listening to a tale of woe only a college student pressured by grades, girls and loneliness can experience. Why the sudden change? It was his child. No one on Earth mattered more to him.

When I am frazzled and call out to God, He responds with total understanding, compassion and love. For I am His child. And so are you.

—ERIC FELLMAN

PRAY: *I pray for _____ today, Father. Convince him/her that You are ready to listen with understanding and compassion at any hour of the day or night.*

DO: Share the story in this devotional with your friend.

WHEN A FRIEND IS HEADED FOR TROUBLE

READ: *For the commandment is a lamp, And the law a light; Reproofs of instruction are the way of life. . . .*

—PROVERBS 6:23

REFLECT: One stormy night a newly commissioned navy captain in his first assignment saw a light moving steadily in the direction of his ship. He ordered the signalman to send the following message: "Change your course ten degrees to the south."

The reply came back: "Change *your* course ten degrees to the north."

The captain was determined not to give way to another vessel, and so he sent a counter message.

"Alter *your* direction ten degrees. I am the captain."

The answer flashed back. "Alter *your* direction. I am a lighthouse!"

There are times when I have allowed self-will to set me off on a collision course. But God, whose Word is like a lighthouse with a penetrating and unchangeable beacon, reveals a rocky shore ahead and I finally do what I am sure that captain did. I obey.

—DORIS HAASE

PRAY: *Lord, my friend doesn't have a clue where the course he/she is on will take him/her. Please give him/her the desire to read the commands in Your Word and obey.*

DO: Give your friend a small lighthouse figurine or picture and tell him/her this story.

WHEN A FRIEND
IS IN A PANIC

◂◦▸

READ: *The Lord will fight for you, and you shall hold your peace.*

—EXODUS 14:14

REFLECT: I was hiking with friends in the Blue Ridge Mountains when our group accidentally stirred up a nest of yellow jackets near the trail. I followed my first instinct and ran.

Then I heard someone yell, "Just hold very still, and move slowly so you don't get stung!" But I continued running rather than follow this absurd-sounding advice and got stung several times. Later, I learned that the man who had advised remaining still had not been stung.

Now, when I grow fearful about something, I employ both parts of that man's advice: *Be still.* I first spend time just listening to God, quieting my anxious thoughts and moving to the deep place within me where God can speak to my fears. Then, *move slowly.* I consider my options carefully, thinking through each possible plan of action to anticipate its outcome. And I remind myself that God is already working in the situation on my behalf. —LISA ISENHOWER

PRAY: *Lord, I want to bring a wise word to those around me in a panic. Would You give me that Word for someone who needs it today?*

DO: Slow down and go to that deep place within you where God can speak to your fears.

WHEN A FRIEND
IS IN DEEP NEED

◄◦►

READ: *"I will be a Father to you, And you shall be My sons and daughters, Says the Lord Almighty.*

—2 CORINTHIANS 6:18

REFLECT: One time when I was little, I was deeply frightened by an event far beyond my comprehension. My father's sister was seriously ill and the family had gathered at her bedside. We children were instructed to remain outdoors.

Not understanding the situation, but sensing its gravity nonetheless, I huddled alone beneath the shade of the big pear tree—until suddenly the quietness seemed overwhelming. Crying out in utter terror, I ran toward the forbidden parlor and its gloom. Immediately a warm, familiar hand closed reassuringly over mine. My father scooped me up into his arms and I knew then that, no matter what, everything was going to be all right—Daddy was with me.

Today, it is not the grief on the faces of those around me at that time that I best recall. It is the tender memory that my father was with me in my time of deepest need.

—JUNE MASTERS BACHER

PRAY: *Loving Comforter, thank You for a lifetime of memories of Your comfort in my hours of deepest need.*

DO: Share a memory of God's comfort to you personally with a friend in need.

WHEN A FRIEND IS LONELY

<o>

READ: *Set your mind on things above, not on things on the earth.*

— COLOSSIANS 3:2

REFLECT: The telephone hadn't rung all day. No one had stopped by. Nothing had come in the mail. My husband was away on a business trip—and I was lonely.

I tried not to think about it because I had plenty of work to do. But every time I stopped typing, I was acutely aware of the silence.

I have friends and loved ones, I thought. *So why do I feel this lonely? Maybe I ought to call them.* So I telephoned a few friends, but no one was home. Finally, in desperation, I closed my eyes and bowed my head. "God," I said, "I'm a little lonely right now—" and I poured out my feelings to Him. Then—after a few tears, a few sighs—a warm, peaceful feeling enveloped me. Yes, Someone does care . . . all the time. I had only to reach out to know that He was right there, constantly there.

— PHYLLIS HOBE

PRAY: *Father, sometimes we feel lonely whether we have good reason to or not. Would You bless _____ today with an awareness of Your constant presence?*

DO: Ask God if any of your friends are feeling lonely today. Pray for, call and/or visit whoever comes to mind.

WHEN A FRIEND IS PHYSICALLY HANDICAPPED

————————◀○▶————————

READ: *We also who have the first fruits of the Spirit, even we ourselves groan within ourselves, eagerly waiting for the adoption, the redemption of our body.*

—ROMANS 8:23

REFLECT: Our newspaper ran a picture of what a six-year-old boy's idea of heaven was like. The child suffered a handicap that kept him indoors, where he sat at the window and watched children playing. He longed to join them.

In childish lines, the picture showed a park crammed with swings, slides and merry-go-rounds. A stick figure that represented the child himself played on everything in the park.

It seems to me that the little boy had grasped the great truth Paul talked about in Romans 8:23 (TLB): "We groan to be released from pain and suffering. We . . . wait anxiously for that day when God will give us our full rights as his children, including the new bodies he has promised us—bodies that will never be sick again and will never die."

Someday all Christians will be released from frustrations and limitations that hold us down in this life!

—SHARI SMITH

PRAY: *I pray, Father, that You would heal _____ in body, mind and spirit.*

DO: Help your friend stay positive through prayer, conversation and/or passing along this story.

WHEN A FRIEND IS PUSHING YOU AWAY

◄○►

READ: *The wolf also shall dwell with the lamb... And a little child shall lead them.*

—ISAIAH 11:6

REFLECT: When he was three, my grandson Caleb loved to play "wolf." He would build a tower of cardboard blocks around himself. I would crawl back and forth in front of the tower, growling, "I'm a big, bad wolf! I'm going to eat you up!" Every time Caleb tried to come out, I'd snap my teeth. Finally he'd burst through the blocks and run into the living room, laughing.

One Saturday, after my knees ached and I'd growled myself hoarse, I changed the rules. I sat down and pretended to cry. "I'm a big, bad wolf! No one will play with me! Won't anyone be my friend?"

Caleb's laughter stopped abruptly. For a moment I thought he would burst into tears. Then he grinned. "Me!" he shouted. "I will be the wolf's friend!" And he launched himself into my arms.

A silly game? Yes, but one that demonstrated a profound truth: Love can often turn a growling wolf into a gentle friend.

—PENNEY SCHWAB

PRAY: *Lord Jesus, help me be a gentle friend to*

_____.

DO: Decide to always be a gentle friend instead of a growling wolf.

WHEN A FRIEND IS TROUBLED

◄◦►

READ: *"It is true! The Lord is risen. . . ."*

—LUKE 24:34

REFLECT: He was so old and wrinkled that it was hard to imagine he had ever been young. He sat on the same bus stop bench every sunny day and watched people come and go, and his lined face seemed alive with an inner joy. *How could anyone so shabby and wrinkled always have such a warm smile?* I wondered.

"You look so happy this morning," I said.

"Why not?" he answered. "Life is good."

"But don't you ever have troubles?" I asked.

"Oh, you can't live a long time and not have troubles," he agreed. "It's just that . . . well, you know the story? How God's Son died on a Cross on Good Friday? Well, just look what happened only three days later! So you see, whenever things go wrong, I've learned to wait three days. Somehow by then, things always seem much better."

—DORIS HAASE

PRAY: *Lord, help my friend see just a few days past the problem he/she is seeing right now.*

DO: Help your friend visualize life after this problem has passed.

WHEN A FRIEND NEEDS A CHANGE OF SCENERY

―――――――――◄○►―――――――――

READ: *When I returned, there, along the bank of the river, were very many trees on one side and the other.*

—EZEKIEL 47:7

REFLECT: During my first years in New York, I lived on a street that had no trees. Not even a blade of grass. I lived on a high floor, and when I looked out my windows all I saw were the backs of other buildings. I got used to this, but now and then I would get the feeling that I was missing something.

Then a friend of mine invited me to spend a weekend at his home in the suburbs. Walking along, old delights struck me. The smell of freshly cut grass. The surprise of a rosebush in bloom. The coolness in the shadows of trees in full leaf.

As soon as I could, I moved—across the street from a park where I could see trees and grass, spring bushes in flower, and, beyond, the Hudson River. It comforted me to know that, in the same way, God is always there. We can see Him, if we try.

—GLENN KITTLER

PRAY: *God, it would do my friend _____ so much good to have a change of scenery. Would You lead him/her to a place where looking out a window can provide a fresh glimpse of You?*

DO: Encourage your friend to look, with faith, for a new place to live.

When a friend
needs a lift

◄○►

READbold: *I . . . will make them rejoice rather than sorrow.*

—JEREMIAH 31:13

REFLECT: It was Monday morning rush hour, and the subway car was a sardine can of half-awake New Yorkers. Trapped and unable to move, I found myself staring into the frowning face of a young woman. As she glanced over my shoulder, the frown vanished and a smile tugged at her lips. The same thing happened to the young man standing next to her and to the old man beside him.

I turned around to see what they were looking at, and I began to smile too. Above the door some graffiti artist had proclaimed:

I LOV EVRY SINGEL BODDY IN THE HOLEWORLD

Kid, I thought, *you can't spell, and you shouldn't write on subway cars, but you certainly have the right idea.*

Walking to my office in the rain, I thought of other sullen moments when a sudden smile or a friendly nod could have chased my inner storms away.
—GLENN KITTLER

PRAY: *God, I definitely don't love "evry singel boddy,"*
often not even my own friends and family the way
I should. I need Your help to brighten their day
with love.

DO: Give a special treat to a special person in your life today.

WHEN A FRIEND
NEEDS COMFORTING

‹○›

READ: *They looked to Him and were radiant,*
And their faces were not ashamed.

—PSALM 34:5

REFLECT: One day, I was lying on the sofa, clutching a box of tissues, suffering from a bad case of allergies. "Here's a hot cup of tea for you, Mom," said my daughter Lauren. "Maybe it will help you feel better." It was such a simple thing, but it warmed my insides and helped relieve my headache. *It's just like so many of God's words,* I thought. How many times had my favorite Psalm comforted me when I was worried or depressed!

Here are some of my favorite "comfort" verses. Often I'll write them on index cards and prop them on my desk.

He will cover you with his feathers, and under his wings you will find refuge (Psalm 91:4).

Now may the Lord of peace himself give you peace at all times and in every way (II Thessalonians 3:16).

The Lord is near to all who call on him . . . (Psalm 145:18).

—ELLEN SECREST

PRAY: *Thank You that the power of Your Word to comfort never changes.*

DO: Design a stack of comfort cards with your handpicked Psalms for a friend.

WHEN A FRIEND
NEEDS FRIENDS

◄○►

READ: *He heals the brokenhearted and binds up their wounds.*

—PSALM 147:3

REFLECT: I longed to get to know the men and women my husband Gene and I met with on Sunday mornings for a Bible study. Our leader announced that those wishing to do so could share a brief testimony about how they came to know and experience God. It took five Sundays.

Underneath the proper clothes and smiling faces were some terribly wounded people. Tears became commonplace, but there was laughter, too, and impromptu hugs as the room seemed to fill with God's unconditional love. People spoke, haltingly but truthfully, about addictions, deception, violation of marriage vows, unforgiveness, promiscuity, violence and abuse, divorce, worry and depression, broken hearts, loneliness, lust and uncontrollable anger.

When the last person had finished, we sat unmoving in total silence, now bonded together by our fierce struggles and amazing survivals. Every one of us, limping badly emotionally and spiritually, had finally run, many of us literally for our lives, into the open arms of Christ the Healer.

—MARION BOND WEST

PRAY: *Father, would You draw people who need healing to Your open arms?*

DO: Invite hurting people to church or to a support group with you.

WHEN A FRIEND
NEEDS HEALING

◄○►

READ: *To him who is afflicted, kindness should be shown by his friend. . . .*

—JOB 6:14

REFLECT: I stared at the bracelet that my wife was wearing: a string of colorful plastic beads that didn't really go with her black dress or the gold chain on her other wrist, but I said nothing.

I noticed it again one evening when Carol was serving dinner. Later, she pushed it up on her forearm as she sat in bed, reading. Finally, I asked, "Why are you wearing that?"

"For Grace," she said, naming a friend who had recently had a nervous breakdown. "She made it as part of her therapy and gave it to me. I promised to wear it until she became well."

About the only time she took it off was to amuse our son Timothy when he became fidgety in church. Then one day it was gone.

"You must miss your bracelet," I said.

"It was a good reminder to pray for Grace, but now I have something better. A friend who's well." —RICK HAMLIN

PRAY: *Lord, thank You for faithful friends and prayer partners. Let me be that for someone who needs it.*

DO: Think of your own creative reminder to pray for those you've said you'll pray for.

WHEN A FRIEND NEEDS PRAYER

◄◦►

READ: *Be ready to give a defense to everyone who asks you a reason for the hope that is in you. . . .*

—I PETER 3:15

REFLECT: I recognized Irene's voice as soon as I picked up the phone. She sounded discouraged. "Papa is sick," she said. Her father, now in his eighties, had been admitted to the hospital.

"I'm so scared," she continued, beginning to cry. I could feel her grief, her fear. She was already missing him. Somehow she knew: Her father would not make it.

I just listened. Irene had come to me for help, but all I could do was pray, and since Irene wasn't one of my Christian friends, I didn't feel comfortable praying with her. Perhaps she'd be embarrassed or offended.

But as I listened to her sobbing, I seemed to hear a deeper cry: *Pray for me! I called you because I knew you would pray.* Her need penetrated my foolish pride, and somehow I found myself praying aloud into the phone. Within minutes, she brightened.

"Thank you so much," she said. "I feel much better." And I did too.

—ROBIN WHITE GOODE

PRAY: *Father, help me always follow Your leading rather than being led by my preconceived opinions.*

DO: Take a chance. Offer to pray for a friend in need you think wouldn't want prayer.

WHEN A LOVED ONE
FEELS HOPELESS

◄◌►

READ: *This hope we have as an anchor of the soul, both sure and steadfast. . . .*

—HEBREWS 6:19

REFLECT: A psychologist once tested thousands of college freshmen on a "hope scale" and found the level of hope a more accurate predictor of future grades than SAT scores. Another psychologist reported that spinal-injury patients with high hope have a far better recovery record than those with identical injuries and low hope.

Vaclav Havel, president of the Czech Republic, expected nothing good when he was imprisoned by his country's Communist regime. Yet he was able to write: "I carry hope in my heart. Hope is a feeling that life and work have meaning . . . whatever the state of the world around you."

"Life without hope," Havel continued, "is an empty, boring and useless life. . . . I am thankful to God for the gift of hope. It is as big a gift as life itself." Hope is a gift of God . . . filling our lives with the assurance of His purpose in good times and in bad.

—ELIZABETH SHERRILL

PRAY: *I pray for _____ today, Lord, that his/her hope would be in You and not circumstances. Restore his/her vision for the future.*

DO: Help your loved one focus on his/her purpose for now and for the future.

When a loved one feels lost and confused

———◄◦►———

READ: *The darkness and the light are both alike to You.*

—PSALM 139:12

REFLECT: Recently my friend Tim accompanied his father to the hospital for a radiation treatment. Cancer is affecting his father's thought processes. As they sat in the waiting room, Tim heard his father quietly pray, "Lord, I don't know why I'm here. I used to know, but now I'm not sure. But I remember that You know why and will help me."

Tim had just accepted a faculty position at a university in a different state. The decision to make this abrupt move had been difficult, and he spent sleepless nights assessing his situation. Sitting in the midst of packing crates in a new house in an unfamiliar city, Tim heard his father's quiet voice: "Lord, I don't know why I'm here. But I remember that You know why and will help me."

Many times have I found myself suddenly not knowing why I am here or where I am going. Yet, like Tim and his father, I have also learned that God knows the way even when I am lost.

—SCOTT WALKER

PRAY: *Lord, I give You my need to understand everything. I choose to trust in Your goodness whether or not I understand all Your plans for my life.*

DO: Pray the above prayer with a loved one who feels lost and confused today.

When a loved one is ill

The divider line with ornament follows.

READ: *The prayer of faith will save the sick, and the Lord will raise him up.*

—JAMES 5:15

REFLECT: Six Christian women of my acquaintance, all over sixty, suffered broken hips within months of each other.

One who was overweight recovered slowly, first on a walker, then on a cane for months before she could walk unsteadily on her own. A second, who was thinner, had a normal recovery and praised the Lord each step of the way. A third, given to depression, recovered slowest of all.

But a fourth, in her nineties, was out of the hospital in less than three weeks, then went home and moved rapidly from walker to cane to walking without any aids.

The key for Number Four was her enthusiasm. She never paused once in self-pity. She spent time praying for Numbers Three, Five and Six. When told that others had been praying for her, she responded glowingly "Why, of course, I could feel it! And it was a powerful instrument in my recovery!"

—SAM JUSTICE

PRAY: *I pray for _____, recovering from surgery today, Lord. Keep him/her from self-pity and help his/her body to heal quickly.*

DO: Write out a prayer and deliver it by hand, mail or e-mail to the friend for whom you just prayed.

WHEN A LOVED ONE
IS IN DANGER

◄◦►

READ: *Peace I leave with you, My peace I give to you....*

—JOHN 14:27

REFLECT: I once interviewed Debbie Dortzbach, the American missionary-nurse who was kidnapped for twenty-six days in Ethiopia. Pregnant at the time of the kidnapping, Debbie now held her young son Joshua (so named because it means "the Lord saves").

"The amazing thing to me was the peace I felt," she told me. "Not an assurance that I wouldn't be killed like Anna (another kidnapped nurse who was shot), but rather the peace that comes from knowing you are Christ's and that He will not forsake you." Such spiritual strength in times of crisis is not a miracle, but rather a residual product of long communion with God. Your best defense in an emergency is to know the Defender, and trust Him. You're in good hands with Him.

—FRED BAUER

PRAY: *God, would You give Your peace and protection to all people who are in harm's way?*

DO: Pray John 14:27, inserting your loved one's name in place of the words *you* and *your*.

WHEN A LOVED ONE IS IN PHYSICAL PAIN

◄○►

READ: *But when He saw the multitudes, He was moved with compassion for them. . . .*

—MATTHEW 9:36

REFLECT: A friend and I, staying at a monastery, had gone for a hike when I felt the pain in my lower back signaling a muscle spasm. I could only walk without pain by bending. It was an odd sight as I came through the monastery door in the perpendicular.

At lunchtime, a shadow crossed in front of me. It was Father Ted. He had bent down into the same position, and we were now nose to nose. "Di," he said with a twinkle in his eye, "could you give me a clue as to the correct pastoral response to your painful situation?"

"Father," I replied, amused, "compassion does not require that you be bent like me." But it certainly was an encouraging starting point.

This was a valuable lesson for me to take home to my medical practice. Compassion is sharing someone else's point of view (even nose to nose). It is always the correct pastoral—and medical—response. —DIANE KOMP

PRAY: *Lord, would You give me compassion so others can feel Your touch through mine?*

DO: Try to see a friend's pain from his/her point of view.

WHEN A LOVED ONE IS IN THE MILITARY

◄◦►

READ: *And she bound the scarlet cord in the window.*

—JOSHUA 2:21

REFLECT: The day our son Chris left for Afghanistan with the Army, my husband Gordon insisted that I buy ribbon to make a gigantic yellow bow. As I tied the bow around the huge pine tree by the driveway, I felt a stab of loneliness.

The next morning, as I was picking up the newspaper, a neighbor stopped. When I told her about Chris, she said, "I'll be praying for him." Soon another neighbor called. "We want to have a cookout to let you know we support your family." At the cookout a seven-year-old girl named Amanda offered me a gift bag. A mother brought her two boys over and each whispered a bit shyly that they were praying for Chris.

The day Chris returned from Afghanistan safe and sound, I took down the yellow ribbon. It was stained and had pine straw stuck in it. I shook out the bow and stored it as a reminder of those who comforted and prayed for us during his absence.

—KAREN BARBER

PRAY: *I pray today for all who are serving in the military. Cover them with Your angels, bless them for their service, and bring them safely home, please, Lord.*

DO: Tie a yellow ribbon around some small something in your home to remind you to pray for our military personnel.

WHEN A LOVED ONE IS LOST

◄o►

READ: *"You are the light of the world. A city that is set on a hill cannot be hidden."*

—MATTHEW 5:14

REFLECT: My sixteen-year-old son John and I were hiking in the rugged Green Mountains in Vermont. The temperature dropped and rain began to fall. In the late afternoon, we finally reached our cabin, then John set off to catch some fish.

An hour later, I woke from a doze to find it was pitch dark, and John hadn't come back. When he didn't answer my repeated calls, I panicked. I lighted candles, then rummaged for a flashlight to go search for my lost son.

Then John burst into the cabin. He had lost his way in the dark and hadn't known what to do—until he saw the light of the flickering candles.

We can help one another by keeping our own light burning: a word of encouragement, a Scripture, a promise to pray. No matter how small, it can lead someone home . . . to the welcoming arms of God.   —JOHN BRAMBLETT

PRAY: *Father, send a light to _____ until he/she finds his/her way to You.*

DO: Send a ray of light to a lost loved one with a word of encouragement, a Scripture, a prayer.

WHEN A LOVED ONE
IS PUSHING YOU AWAY

◄○►

READ: *Jesus said, "Father, forgive them, for they do not know what they do."*

—LUKE 23:34

REFLECT: My fourteen-year-old son's greatest delight seemed to be teasing his sister Jana, who was eleven. The taunts and comments led to bickering and frequently to tears.

One day when the teasing became too much for her, Jana screamed in a voice loud enough to be heard throughout the house, "I love you, Alan. Sometimes you try to keep me from it. But you can't stop me from loving you." With tears streaming down her face, she fled to her room, leaving Alan speechless.

Sometimes God speaks loudly to us so that we stop and listen. I think of the death of Jesus on the cross as a silent scream of God in which He says, "I love you that much, no matter what you do."

—RUTH DINKINS ROWAN

PRAY: *Thank You, Father, for people who love me even when I give them every reason not to.*

DO: Do something kind for an unkind loved one.

WHEN A LOVED ONE IS STRUGGLING

<o>

READ: *Wisdom is the principal thing; Therefore get wisdom. And in all your getting, get understanding.*

—PROVERBS 4:7

REFLECT: I was on the telephone, a long way from home, dealing with a school crisis my son was having. He shouted, "I hate it, Dad! Hate it, hate it, hate it!" Then he slammed down the receiver.

Helpless to call him back because he was calling from a pay phone, I took a walk around the neighborhood where I was staying. As I passed a vacant lot, the piercing cry of a killdeer caught my attention. I walked toward the bird and watched in fascination as it flopped through the grass, apparently the victim of a broken wing.

I laughed, recalling the "broken wing" trick killdeer use to keep intruders away from what is really important—their nests. Maybe my son was using a "broken wing" to deflect my attention from the real problem. Later that night we talked, and I listened for what was really bothering him: insecurity at making friends and finding his place.

The next time you face a strong emotional response, look closely at the "broken wing" and listen for the real problem.

—ERIC FELLMAN

PRAY: *Lord, give me ears to hear, eyes to see and a heart to understand what is behind the pain I see today in other people's lives.*

DO: Consider the killdeer trick during your own extreme emotional responses.

WHEN A LOVED ONE
IS SUFFERING A LOSS

◄○►

READ: *We know that we have passed from death to life, because we love our brothers.*

—1 JOHN 3:14 (NIV)

REFLECT: One day I was getting into my car when I noticed absentmindedly that our four-year-old daughter was playing near the driveway with her dolly. But my mind was already at the office as I started the engine, looked in the rearview mirror and backed the car out of the garage. Suddenly, I heard a snapping crunch, then a scream. My stomach knotted and my throat tightened as I jumped out of the car.

My daughter was standing beside the car, her shattered doll in her arms, sobbing. And through her tears came rage and hurt. "You've killed my baby!" she shouted. She would not be consoled.

As painful as it was, it would give my daughter some of the experience she would need to deal with grief as an adult. Maybe, I thought, from God's perspective we adults are like four-year-olds, and perhaps a firsthand knowledge of sickness and death is necessary for us if we are to enter into the sufferings of others.

—KEITH MILLER

PRAY: *Dear Lord, thank You for the cross, through which You have shared—somehow joined me—in my suffering. Help me to use my own crosses to grow in love.*

DO: Make yourself available to a share a friend's grief.

WHEN A LOVED ONE IS SUFFERING FROM ALZHEIMER'S

<o>

READ: *Let not your heart be troubled, neither let it be afraid.*

—JOHN 14:27

REFLECT: My wife Ruth and I had lunch with a distinguished doctor who devoted his life to the study of chronic pain. During his research, he made an amazing discovery about chronic pain in patients who also suffered symptoms of Alzheimer's disease.

"I found that sensitivity to various kinds of chronic pain was greatly reduced in patients with Alzheimer's," he told us. "We could find no organic reason for this pattern. My conclusion, based on the medical and psychological evidence, is that memory loss reduces pain.

"The patient's inability to remember yesterday's pain, or to anticipate tomorrow's, greatly reduced the current effect of pain."

I was tremendously intrigued by this scientific evidence of a biblical principle. Just think of how many of life's hurts could be eliminated if we could forget yesterday and not anticipate tomorrow. Face only today. Yesterday is over, and tomorrow will take care of itself.

—NORMAN VINCENT PEALE

PRAY: *I pray for_____ today, Lord, and ask You to protect him/her from the pain of yesterday, today and tomorrow.*

DO: Pray for patience for yourself as you serve a loved one with Alzheimer's.

WHEN A LOVED ONE
NEEDS HELP

READ: *Whoever keeps the fig tree will eat its fruit. . . .*

—PROVERBS 27:18

REFLECT: The last time Dad had been to church he had driven his car and walked into the service. This time we pushed him in a wheelchair after a difficult recovery from stomach surgery.

We headed straight for Dad's customary place in the sanctuary—a special bench in a small alcove near a side door. Dad had helped put the bench there seven years earlier when my mother needed a wheelchair after a stroke. Now Mom was gone, and it was Dad in the wheelchair.

I felt the solid bench underneath me. Dad's years of faithfulness to Mom had become the means through which God, in turn, showed His faithfulness to Dad. He had been there Sunday after Sunday, making the bench a comfortable place for the disabled to worship.

I suppose that's the way it is with those who faithfully serve and give. They never guess how their acts of kindness will be returned to them in their own time of need.

—KAREN BARBER

PRAY: *Dear Father, thank You that our small acts of service have a way of returning to us.*

DO: Contribute to a service project that has special meaning for you or someone you love.

WHEN A LOVED ONE WORKS IN THE FINANCIAL WORLD

<o>

READ: *Let your speech always be with grace, seasoned with salt, that you may know how you ought to answer each one.*

—COLOSSIANS 4:6

REFLECT: My twenty-three-year-old son Tim is a tender young man in the tough business of New York finance. As a junior analyst at a mutual fund company, he works sixteen-hour days fielding hundreds of phone calls from brokers, traders and clients who are more volatile than the stock market. His new profession operates through open conflict, and he's been yelled at, harangued, threatened and hung up on. And yet, despite—or perhaps because of—his quiet nature, he has prospered. He has brought in new customers, shepherded sensitive negotiations to their successful conclusions while earning the respect of seasoned and senior associates.

"How do you do it?" I recently asked him, amazed that the gentle boy of memory could go one-on-one with hard-boiled, aggressive types.

"When somebody yells, I speak more softly," he replied. "If people throw tantrums, I keep my cool. If they're rude, I'm pointedly polite. They don't know what to do with me. Eventually, they wind up listening."

—LINDA CHING SLEDGE

PRAY: *Lord, please let _____ 's speech be seasoned with grace during these tumultuous financial times.*

DO: Don't just tell your financial analyst friend that you are praying for him/her. Do it right then and there.

WHEN A NEIGHBOR
HAS A NEED

<o>

READ: *"Here am I! Send me."*

—ISAIAH 6:8

REFLECT: One June, just after disastrous tornadoes had swirled through Ohio, Pennsylvania and Ontario, a woman on television said something that affected me deeply. The camera showed her surrounded by men in large, black flat-rimmed hats, clearing debris, hauling lumber, rebuilding wrecked homes. These men were members of the Amish sect. They had come en masse, by buggy and by bus, to help the people—strangers to them—who were in distress. Their presence was not surprising, for with the Amish, helping others is a tradition, a way of life.

"When the Amish came," the woman on television said, "it was as though God had reached down with His own helping Hand."

I looked at my hand, and I saw it in a way I had never seen it before. Have you ever thought, just as I did then, of your hand as God's helping Hand?

—RUTH STAFFORD PEALE

PRAY: *Father, use my hands as Your hands to help others.*

DO: Volunteer to help a neighbor, or someone in your own household, in need today.

When an inner storm is raging

◄◎►

READ: *He calms the storm, So that its waves are still.*

—PSALM 107:29

REFLECT: A storm howled outside the concert hall, as inner turmoil raged within me. Money problems, an argument with my wife and a friend's acid comments about my competitive nature bombarded me. My attention then turned to the soloist, whose lovely voice filled the hall. Her ease of manner was attractive, and her face glowed as she sang. For the moment, I forgot about the storm.

After the performance, I made my way through the guests to congratulate the soloist. I was amazed to see that she was supported by two metal crutches grasping her forearms! But her handicap didn't dampen her enthusiasm for music or for life. "I was a music teacher before my hip problem," she told me, "but now I sing all the time." She had risen above her illness to enrich others' lives.

I could use God's gift—be it a financial problem, a handicap or even a crisis—to quell any storms I might face.

—OSCAR GREENE

PRAY: *Father, I receive my problems as gifts from You to enrich others' lives.*

DO: Ask how you can help a friend with a problem similar to what you're facing . . . or ask for his/her advice.

WHEN CONTRARY WINDS OF LIFE ARE BLOWING

———◀◦▶———

READ: *The wind blows where it wishes, and you hear the sound of it, but cannot tell where it comes from and where it goes.*

—JOHN 3:8

REFLECT: One year my husband realized a childhood ambition of learning to sail. He took three lessons and then bought a used sailboat. We had wonderful times sailing when we lived in New York—and then Kentucky—with our three small children and Trixie the beagle.

One of the things that surprised me most about sailing was that the same wind could take the boat in almost all directions. It depended on where I steered with the rudder and how I set the sails.

I'm trying to apply this principle to the rest of my life. I can't control the winds that blow, but with God's help I can set my sails accordingly. I can look for the beauty in people who treat me unfairly. I can try to counter criticism with affirmation. Even contrary winds can be used by God to teach me something new. —BARBARA CHAFIN

PRAY: *Father, just because contrary winds are blowing in my life doesn't mean I have to be contrary too. Help me to set my sails to make the most of those winds.*

DO: Get a toy bathtub sailboat to remind you how to respond when contrary winds are blowing against you.

WHEN CREATIVITY WON'T COME

◄◦►

READ: *God created man in His own image. . . .*

—GENESIS 1:27

REFLECT: "You can make anything you want," the teacher said, placing jars of paint in the center of each table. I watched as the preschoolers began swiping and swirling the colors across their papers.

When the pictures were done, we arranged them along the wall: a strawberry tree; a blue dog; a lady with six hands, "because my mommy's always saying she needs more hands!" I was impressed that each drawing was unique. Such creativity!

I thought about my own life. How routine it had become! I made the same meatloaf, drove the same routes, prayed the same phrases. I even made the same mistakes.

God is the great Creator—and we are His children, made in His image. Creativity is our heritage! Yet often we face both our opportunities and our problems with tunnel vision. Creativity enables us to see things in new ways, to produce original solutions, to break out of the "but-we've-always-done-it-this-way" rut.

—MARY LOU CARNEY

PRAY: *Holy Spirit, I want to do things the-way-we've-never-done-it way. Would You give me ideas how?*

DO: Try to do the usual tasks in your life in an unusual way.

WHEN FEAR ATTACKS YOUR FAITH

READ: *Now in the fourth watch of the night Jesus went to them, walking on the sea.*

—MATTHEW 14:25

REFLECT: On a visit South, a friend and I drove along the New Orleans Gulf Coast. Gazing out over the huge body of shimmering water, I observed three people in the distance—walking on its surface!

"But that's impossible!" I gasped.

My companion laughed. "The water barely covers a mile-wide shelf of rock and is only a foot or two deep. So you see," he said, "there's a logical explanation for everything."

Not quite everything, I thought, remembering Jesus' disciples. They had no logical explanation when they saw Jesus walking toward them on the Sea of Galilee. They had only faith. In fact, Peter walked on the water toward his Master—until fear caused him to sink (Matthew 14:30).

Sometimes fear attacks my faith too, and I think I might sink into despair, but when I cry "Lord, save me!" Jesus always stretches out His hand. —DORIS HAASE

PRAY: *Jesus, give me faith like Peter's in Your power to save.*

DO: Stretch out your hand to a friend whose faith is failing.

WHEN FEAR THREATENS TO CONTROL YOU

READ: *Be strong and of good courage. . . .*
— DEUTERONOMY 31:6

REFLECT: When my boss told me I had to give a speech before our managers, I broke out in a cold sweat. I was tempted to say, "I can't do it," but my boss's confidence kept me silent. When the big day arrived, I managed to get through my talk, even though my voice sounded creaky. I was sure my one joke fell flat, and when one man asked a question, I stammered through the answer.

Finally, the managers left and my boss revealed that he had videotaped my presentation! I actually looked and sounded a lot more composed than I felt. "Now," he said, "aren't you glad you didn't let your fear stop you?"

I'm sure God doesn't want fear to stop me from doing what He knows I can do. Maybe He uses it as a spur to get me to work as hard as I can. — LINDA NEUKRUG

PRAY: *I'm grateful, Father, for people who believe in me when I don't believe in myself.*

DO: Challenge a friend to say yes to a new experience that will stretch him/her.

WHEN GOD IS DOING WONDERFUL THINGS FOR YOU

READ: *Though the fig tree may not blossom, nor fruit be on the vines ... yet I will rejoice in the Lord.*

—HABAKKUK 3:17–18

REFLECT: My husband had a new job and I bubbled to everyone about the marvelous things God was doing for us.

Then a very wise man stopped me. "I praise God for what He is doing in your life, Patti. But remember: When God did the best thing He ever did for us, it was very painful."

It is easy for us as Christians to accept God's work in our lives as a process that provides us with continual bliss. But if we are honest, we have to admit that our lives are not free from pain.

God has not promised to make our lives easy. He has promised that we will never be called upon to endure more than we can bear. And He *has* promised that He will go through every experience with us.

—PATRICIA HOUCK SPRINKLE

PRAY: *Lord Jesus, never let me forget that the greatest thing You ever did for us was very painful. Help me to embrace the hard things in life and find Your purpose in them.*

DO: Print this devotional and tuck it into your Bible as a reminder to be grateful for life's next challenge.

WHEN GOD SAYS *NO* TO YOUR PRAYER

READ: *Rest in the Lord, and wait patiently for Him. . . .*

—PSALM 37:7

REFLECT: When I was sixteen, I fell in love. Although I knew in a short while it wasn't meant to be—he was a few years older, and we were from different worlds—my heart would have no part of it. I was convinced that I would never again feel the same way about another human being. In my innocence, I prayed that God would correct all the problems and give me the desire of my heart. For two years, I repeated that prayer, wondering why God wasn't answering.

I confessed my despair to my brother-in-law Marion. "Be patient, Libbie," he said. "You'll probably end up marrying someone you haven't even met yet." That wasn't what I wanted to hear.

But by the following year, Marion's prediction had come true: I had met the man I've spent thirty-one years with, and who truly is the desire of my heart. And I'm grateful that God loved me enough to say no when I was asking Him for all the wrong things.

—LIBBIE ADAMS

PRAY: *For all the times You said no because You know what is best for me, thank You.*

DO: Comfort a friend who is disappointed with God's answer to his/her prayer by sending this story.

WHEN HELP COMES UNEXPECTEDLY

<hr>

READ: *He who does good is of God. . . .*

—3 JOHN 11

REFLECT: One freezing night during basic training, my buddy and I tried in vain to hammer our wooden tent pegs into the crusty ground. We struggled on, thinking of the cold night ahead, managing only to break another wooden peg.

Then someone said over my shoulder, "You guys look like you could use a little help."

He was tall, dressed in the same army-issue clothing. He had a small sledgehammer and six brand-new metal tent pegs. It took him no more than a minute to set up our tent, then he moved on.

"I was praying for help," Jack muttered, "but I never expected an angel."

I believe the tent-peg man *was* an angel. We never saw him again, and no one could account for his presence that night.

Years later, I did someone an anonymous favor—small, but significant to the person it helped. So, stay alert. You might have been helped by an angel. And you might be called upon to be one.

—JAMES MCDERMOTT

PRAY: *Provide help to those struggling to get the job done, especially those who wouldn't think to ask for it.*

DO: Offer a hand to someone who clearly needs it.

WHEN IT'S TIME TO LET GO OF YOUR CHILDREN

———◄○►———

READ: *She got a papyrus basket for him and coated it with tar and pitch. Then she placed the child in it and put it among the reeds along the bank of the Nile.*

—EXODUS 2:3 (NIV)

REFLECT: "I don't need any help from y'all. I'm paying for my own college. I've gotten a full-time job. This way, you can't keep butting into my life." Our stubborn daughter packed up her clothes without looking up.

I hugged her stiff body good-bye and didn't walk with her to her car. For weeks, my thoughts went over that scene from every possible angle. I worried about all the things that could happen to her and all the bad choices she might make. One morning, I finally got real with God: "Could You please show me how to let her go?"

A Bible story came to me—the incredible faith of Moses' mother. To save her son, she had no choice but to trust God completely and let him go. Knowing all about the dangers of the dark Nile—crocodiles, drowning, starvation—she still turned him loose in his little handmade basket. And I bet that sweet mama let her son go with hope.

—JULIE GARMON

PRAY: *Father, I place my grown-up baby in the Nile. Only You can follow him/her along the riverbank.*

DO: Read Exodus 2:1–10 and think of the purposes for your child's life that might be accomplished by your letting go.

WHEN LIFE DOESN'T GO ACCORDING TO YOUR PLANS

◄○►

READ: *A man's heart plans his way, But the Lord directs his steps.*

—PROVERBS 16:9

REFLECT: I'm a planner, my mother is a planner and her mother is too. We like to know what's going to happen when. So I struggled when we put our house on the market and it still hadn't sold months later. School was ending, and we wanted to be settled into our new house before the new school year.

My mind raced: *What if we don't sell in time? We can't afford two mortgages. Should I start packing, so we're ready to go as soon as it sells? Or will I look like a fool if I've packed and we end up staying?*

Finally, I talked things over with a wise friend. "Try taking things a day at a time," she suggested, "Ask God each morning what He wants you to accomplish that day." And wouldn't you know it? We got a contract on our house just two weeks after school ended, leaving us time to find a house and get settled before the school year started again.

—WENDY WILLARD

PRAY: *Oh, Lord, remind my planning brain not to get ahead of the plans that You place in my heart each day.*

DO: Ask God what He wants you to accomplish today.

WHEN LIFE FEELS DULL

---◀◎▶---

READ: *He who observes the wind will not sow,*
And he who regards the clouds will not reap.

—ECCLESIASTES 11:4

REFLECT: As a boy I lived in a small, dull town. A massive pine tree there pointed to the clouds as if to say, "This way to adventure." Naturally, one day I obeyed the invitation, clawing my way up until my heart raced. Then I realized that I was much higher than I had thought. I was terrified. Tears came to my eyes, and I prayed fervently, "Please get me down and I will never do this again."

I managed to get down and, for a few days, stayed at a safe level. But something was missing. Danger. Excitement. Gradually, I started to climb higher again, and the thrill came back.

We humans need both security and adventure, but the need for adventure may well be the greater one. When life is perfectly safe it can also be perfectly dull. I try always to climb a little higher than I think I can, and I seldom regret it.

—DANIEL SCHANTZ

PRAY: *God, would You give me vision beyond my ability to accomplish without You?*

DO: Try something that scares you just enough to make your heart race.

WHEN LIFE FEELS LIKE AN EARTHQUAKE

◄○►

READ: *Therefore we will not fear . . . though the earth be removed, and though the mountains be carried into the midst of the sea. . . .*

—PSALM 46:2–3

REFLECT: My friend Jeri had a terrifying experience at a conference in California. "I was on the ninth floor of a hotel when, in the middle of the night, I awoke to find the room swaying! Things were falling off the dresser. I could hear cracking sounds all around."

Jeri, being a Southern gal, was unprepared to be in an earthquake. She made her way to the lobby, along with dozens of other terrified occupants. *Should they leave the hotel? Was it going to come crashing down on them?*

But the manager smiled, passed out coffee and told them that the hotel was safe. "It's built on rollers," he assured them. "We roll with the rhythms of the quake."

Built on rollers. What a perfect description of the life of faith! While not immune to sickness or difficulties, I can stand firm because faith allows me to "roll" instead of crumble in crises. Steadied by the assurance of God's help, I, too, am built to withstand quakes.

—MARY LOU CARNEY

PRAY: *Give us faith, Lord, that allows us to roll with life's difficulties rather than crumble beneath them.*

DO: Find Scriptures to steady you when life begins to feel like an earthquake.

When life feels unfair

—◆◇◆—

READ: *For to everyone who has, more will be given, and he will have abundance. . . .*

—MATTHEW 25:29

REFLECT: "My folks couldn't afford to buy me a bicycle," John Havlicek, Boston Celtic basketball great, once told me, "and I felt cheated. I ran everywhere—to school, to deliver groceries, to basketball practice. I suppose all that running helped me to develop my legs and my stamina."

Interesting. Those who enjoy the finer points of basketball know that movement without the ball is one of the keys to success in the game. The player who keeps running can eventually elude his guard, receive the ball and score. John Havlicek was perpetual motion personified. The lack of a bike when he was a youngster may have aided the development of those sturdy legs that ran other teams ragged.

—FRED BAUER

PRAY: *Thank You, Lord, for preparing me for life by making something positive out of what I thought was negative.*

DO: Help a friend see past the struggle to the positive God could bring out of it.

WHEN LIFE IS A HASSLE

❖

READ: *Mark the blameless man; and observe the upright;*
For the future of that man is peace.

—PSALM 37:37

REFLECT: It was a two-handkerchief book. Evil men tried to cause her downfall; friends betrayed her; happiness seemed to elude her on every page. But still she pursued her dreams—resolute, honorable. And in the end, when I was almost overcome with pity for her, she succeeded. True love prevailed; evil was swallowed by its own sinister schemes. A happy ending!

Sometimes my life seems like that book. Things don't go the way I want. My car battery dies—on the exit ramp of the freeway. My "perfect" dinner turns out charred. The dog slips his collar and disappears. A co-worker gets the job I wanted. I pray for things that never come.

That's when I remind myself that the hassles of day-to-day living are only one part of my story. There's a closing chapter I haven't seen yet, one in which good triumphs finally and forever. A happy ending planned by the Author especially for me!

—MARY LOU CARNEY

PRAY: *Father, remind me to enjoy every chapter of my life,*
not just look forward to the happy ending with You
that I know is coming.

DO: Read a favorite book with a happy ending.

WHEN LIFE IS SHATTERED IN PIECES

◄○►

READ: *You . . . shall revive me again. . . .*

—PSALM 71:20

REFLECT: During World War II the beautiful rose window of a French cathedral was shattered by bombs. The parishioners were saddened by their loss; but the old men who were left in the village, together with the women and children, carefully gathered every fragment of glass they could find.

For days sensitive fingers swept along the ground and searched among the rubble for bits and shards. So dedicated and thorough were they that eventually other skilled hands were able to put all the tiny pieces back together and make the window whole again.

How wonderful it is to know that there is Someone Who reaches down and gathers up the pieces of my life when I have allowed anger, jealousy, bitterness or any of the other destroyers to shatter me. What solace it is to know that His loving hands can put the pieces together again.

—DRUE DUKE

PRAY: *I know You can restore lives, Father, because You restored mine. I pray Your love will show through those whose lives You've restored.*

DO: Search online for directions on how to make your own mosaic as a reminder of God's redeeming power.

WHEN LIFE IS STORMY

◄○►

READ: *We are hard-pressed on every side, yet not crushed; we are perplexed, but not in despair. . . .*

—2 CORINTHIANS 4:8

REFLECT: I read a news article about tornadoes and floods in California, where many homes had been washed away and lives had been lost. One picture showed a Los Angeles street strewn with debris, and in the background stood a storm-damaged building with a sign proclaiming, "Jesus Loves You." Everything else seemed to have given way to the storm—but the sign stood firm.

Could anyone really believe those words while watching their home float away? I wondered. Then I recalled stormy situations in my own life when disappointments had almost overwhelmed me. At those times the love of Jesus was the only thing keeping me from being washed away into total despair.

No matter what raging elements we may have to face, or how grave the loss or damage, our most valuable possession—the only one that will forever withstand life's ravages—is our life in Christ. And that we can never lose.

—SAMANTHA MCGARRITY

PRAY: *Father God, forgive me for thinking that something bad happening means You're not a good God.*

DO: Remind a friend who is accusing God for a storm that God is his/her safest, most loving shelter.

WHEN LIFE SEEMS DARK

◄○►

READ: *The day is Yours, the night also is Yours....*
—PSALM 74:16

REFLECT: Since early childhood, I have been afraid of the dark. As a youngster, I always sent my little sister before me to turn on the light—and as an adult, I prefer bedrooms where streetlights are shining in the window. Whenever I am in total darkness, I encourage myself by repeating a line from George MacDonald: "But the dark is still God!" I hold on to those words until I find the light.

Maybe you don't fear actual darkness as I do. But life has many kinds of darkness—times of uncertainty, times of grief, times of pain and despair. To all of us, these kinds of darkness are bound to bring fear.

Isn't it comforting, then, when we find ourselves in the dark, to know that God created the dark as well as the light—and that He lovingly resides in both?

—PATRICIA HOUCK SPRINKLE

PRAY: *God, be with me in my darkness until it passes.*

DO: Enter into a friend's darkness with gifts, your prayers and/or your presence.

WHEN RELATIONSHIPS ARE STRAINED

<o>

READ: *This I pray, that your love may abound still more and more in knowledge and all discernment. . . .*

—PHILIPPIANS 1:9

REFLECT: Our daughter was living at home again after two years of college, and in some ways it was hard on all of us. She was straining for independence, and we seemed to go from one crisis to another, with her dad and me often feeling bewildered. Each day I'd prayed for patience, but it hadn't come.

Then one day I heard our minister say something that hit home. He was discussing difficult family relationships. "Don't pray for more patience," he said, "pray for more love."

That very day I began praying not for my kind of love, but for God's love to flow through me to this child of ours.

I really think things are better now. Why? Because our own love is somehow so limited, so judging, so demanding, so fearful. But when God's love is given, through us, to another, there are no such boundaries.

—MAY SHERIDAN GOLD

PRAY: *Forgive me, Father, for my limited, judging, demanding love. Please give me more of Your love for others.*

DO: Ask God to show you when your love has been limited, judging and/or demanding.

WHEN SERVING ISN'T CONVENIENT

READ: *Now may our God and Father himself and our Lord Jesus clear the way for us to come to you.*

—I THESSALONIANS 3:11 (NIV)

REFLECT: I grew up in a quaint Concord grape area on the shores of Lake Erie. As a preteen, I often would pick with my mother, a pleasant way to earn a little money.

I was not an efficient picker, though. I would spend five minutes carefully trimming away leaves from the vines. Troublesome leaves gone, I would nip the few clusters of grapes and move on.

"Kath," Mama would say, "don't pay attention to the leaves. There are too many. Reach right past them and get your grapes."

Today I find I still fuss with the leaves. I put off visiting an ailing elder because of a dirty kitchen floor or a car rattle. I can't attend prayer meetings because I'm too tired, or the clothes need folding.

Oh, the annoying, cluttering leaves of inconvenience! I see that I am going to have to reach right past them and get to the worthwhile fruit. —KATHIE KANIA

PRAY: *Father, I'm great at making excuses, not so great at serving. But I want to be like You Lord, a servant first.*

DO: Clear a regular time on your calendar for serving so you don't have to make time.

WHEN SOMEONE DOESN'T SEEM TO LIKE YOU

<o>

READ: *"Love your enemies, do good to those who hate you, bless those who curse you, and pray for those who spitefully use you."*

—LUKE 6:27–28

REFLECT: John flew out of his ballet rehearsal looking as if he was two seconds from exploding. "I don't like that girl!" he sputtered. I handed him his snack.

"Do you need to talk?" I asked as blandly as possible.

"No!" he shouted and tore up the stairs to sit by the doorway, alone.

After a few minutes I ventured up to ask, "Can you control your feelings until the end of rehearsal?" John scowled but nodded. I sent up a prayer and went back to the waiting area. Soon John returned to the rehearsal studio.

I had a pretty good hunch what was going on. A young but talented dancer was looking at John's struggles with disdain.

Much to my astonishment, John came out of rehearsal beaming. "You look happy!" I commented, baffled.

"Yup. I figured the best thing to do was make friends with her. So I did." John replied.

My son called cheerfully to the troublesome girl. She smiled and waved back.

—JULIA ATTAWAY

PRAY: *Wow, Lord, could You teach me some more ways to love my enemies?*

DO: Make a friend of an enemy!

When someone has been rude to you

READ: *Do to others as you would have them do to you.*

—LUKE 6:31 (NIV)

REFLECT: My stepfather has very good manners, and in today's world they're noticeable. He stands up when a woman enters a room; he writes thank-you notes and even tips his hat.

When my stepdad first came to live with me, my friends were always telling him, "Oh, don't bother to get up, Ray," or "You don't have to do that, Ray." They meant well. He walks with a quad cane and has arthritis, so it takes him a little time to stand up. Nevertheless, he stuck to his good manners.

I've noticed that my dad's good manners are rubbing off on all of us. I even received a thank-you note from a neighbor's son. In fact, he was the one who explained our increasing politeness. "I like the way Ray treats people," Jeff told me. "He makes me feel special."

Good manners are a way of telling someone, "I acknowledge your value as a human being—God's creation."

—PHYLLIS HOBE

PRAY: *Lord God, I pray that my good manners today will make others feel special.*

DO: Teach your child(ren) that good manners never go out of style.

When something has ruined your day

◄○►

READ: *This is the day the Lord has made;*
We will rejoice and be glad in it.

—PSALM 118:24

REFLECT: I was sipping a cup of coffee while leafing through my album of antique postcards when the cup slipped and spilled coffee all over the cards. My sister Rebekkah ran to get a roll of paper towels. As she sopped up the coffee, she said softly, "Don't let it ruin your day, Roberta."

Don't let it ruin your day. Almost always, I would have let that little accident color every remaining moment of the day. *Why did you have to have that coffee in the first place?* I'd have berated myself. How many days had I sacrificed to such regrets?

The cards cost little more than a dollar apiece and were replaceable. But a day the Lord has made? Absolutely priceless. A day full of things to see and do, a day touched with the presence of God in every moment.

Thanks to Rebekkah, I'll never look at an ordinary day in the same way, including the ones that don't go quite the way I'd like.

—ROBERTA MESSNER

PRAY: *Today, Lord, is part of Your divine design. Help me to get out of it everything You intended.*

DO: Look for the positive in a mishap that threatens to ruin your day.

When the Bible seems dry and meaningless

---◇---

READ: *"The Lord is in His holy temple. Let all the earth keep silence before Him."*

—HABAKKUK 2:20

REFLECT: There are days when I open my Bible to read and fall into a desert. This morning I was standing outside the walls of Jerusalem with the fiery prophet Jeremiah, lambasting the callous high priest. The biblical scene, set in an ancient world six hundred years before the birth of Christ, seemed foreign and irrelevant to my life and needs. I nearly stopped reading. I did not want to stroll through the arid dust of history.

When I finished my Bible reading and wrote in my journal, I found these words flowing across the page: "Sometimes I read the Bible and there is nothing there. Only silence. Yet, even in that still silence I am strengthened; I am drawn to a holy presence. It's like two good friends who sit quietly alone, content in each other's company."

God is such a friend. He does not speak at my demand. But as I grow older, I find I need less of His voice and more of His presence. Just to know that He is with me is enough.

—SCOTT WALKER

PRAY: *Dear Father, I'll be still with You today.*

DO: Read what you would normally consider a dry and meaningless portion of Scripture. See what relevancy to your life you can find in it.

WHEN THE DAILY NEWS IS GETTING YOU DOWN

◄◦►

READ: *You will hear of wars and rumors of wars.*

—MATTHEW 24:6

REFLECT: At a conference in upstate New York, I was getting a prebreakfast mug of coffee and listening to the news blaring from the lobby TV. That's when I spotted my old friend Andrew Foster, pastor of the Church of The Ascension in New York City, who was attending a conference at the same hotel. We exchanged how-are-yous, and for once I told him. "Oh, you know, there's so much trouble in the world I don't even know how to pray anymore."

"I used to fall into that trap, too, but no more," said Andrew. "I've put myself on a strict news fast until noon."

A *news fast*. How those two words have changed my life! Today, I listen to the birds, feed a chipmunk, read Scripture and wait till noon to catch up with the latest tragedy. By starting the day with the calm that comes from listening first to God, I cope more successfully with my own problems and see my role in the larger problems around me.

—JOHN SHERRILL

PRAY: *Thank You, Father, for granting me time each day to look at the world from the perspective of eternity.*

DO: Turn off the TV, radio or Internet until after noon and start your day focusing on God.

WHEN THE NEST
IS NEWLY EMPTY

◄○►

READ: *He is before all things, and in Him all things consist.*

—COLOSSIANS 1:17

REFLECT: My eighteen-year-old daughter Tamara is standing at the airport gate, toting a travel bag and blurting, "Oh, this is so exciting!" Her flight is called, and our firstborn is winging off to college.

Why isn't this day so exciting for me? Am I resisting the day because it is forcing me to face change? A lifestyle I have known is shifting down. Will I have a purpose in life other than motherhood?

I bring to the Lord my uncertainties. He answers: "Have you forgotten, Carol, that I am the way and the truth and the life?" (John 14:6).

I get the message. My life is centered in Jesus Christ, not in my children, and not in my future. He is the One directing me—to a new friendship, a hidden talent, an unexpected avenue of service. In every stopover I learn to know myself and I have the incredible privilege of learning to know the living God. What an exciting trip!

—CAROL KNAPP

PRAY: *Jesus, You are my purpose—past, present and future. I live to know more about You.*

DO: Search your Bible to discover something you never before knew about God's character.

WHEN THE WORLD
ASSAILS YOU

◄○►

READ: *"In returning and rest you shall be saved;*
In quietness and confidence shall be your strength."

—ISAIAH 30:15

REFLECT: One unexpected "pleasure" of country living is dealing with all the critters who leap, creep, crawl or fly into our house. Stretched across the corner under our second-story eaves was an intricate spider web. In the center of its eighteen-inch span was perched its creator.

Since it was out of my reach, I hooked up the garden hose to dispel the intruder. But no matter how much I sprayed, the web and its creator came out unscathed. Although it appeared fragile, the web was amazingly strong and elastic. The more force used against it, the more it gave.

I could have used a ladder and won the battle with a broom, but I decided to leave my friend in place as a reminder to relax when the pressures come flying. Instead of fighting back when people or circumstances assail me, I'll try to cling to the threads of confidence and hope that God has built into my life.

—ERIC FELLMAN

PRAY: *Help me be a spider, Lord, clinging to the threads of*
confidence and hope that You have built into my life.

DO: Study the properties of a spider web, up close and personal. If that isn't possible, look it up online and compare them to your spiritual life.

When the World Seems to Be Spinning Out of Control

READ: *The earth is the Lord's, and all its fullness, The world and those who dwell therein.*

—PSALM 24:1

REFLECT: The world according to the morning paper fills me with a sense of doom. It is spinning out of control. *Lord, where is the hope?*

Across my long porch, a male finch perches on the edge of a hanging fern. Grabbing my binoculars, I look inside the fern at the tiny nest cradling three pale blue eggs that have somehow survived cat-stalking, storms and a bird of prey. I watch the plain, brown female pecking at the eggs. *They're hatching!*

I wait awhile, then climb on a railing. The hatchlings are twined together, the size of a nickel. Their parents are hovering nearby to nurture their brood, so they can grow up and fly and sing their song.

Here, in this little backyard miracle, I see the hand that holds the world. An event too ordinary to make the morning paper. But, light as a feather, soft as a whisper, its good news lands in my soul. God is in control.   —SHARI SMYTH

PRAY: *Creator God, thank You for the works of Your hand that give me hope for all the world.*

DO: Find a bird's nest and experience the hope of new birth.

WHEN THERE IS NO ROOM FOR GOD IN YOUR LIFE

◄◦►

READ: *Be still before the Lord. . . .*

—ZECHARIAH 2:13 (NIV)

REFLECT: When the youngest of our three children entered college, my wife Sally and I rattled around our empty house. We could spend a Saturday afternoon working around the house and hardly see each other.

When we went to Africa we lived in a thatched-roof hut barely ten feet in diameter. Movement always involved saying, "Excuse me" and "Can you get by?" We almost had to embrace so that the other could pass! In the mornings, we delayed meeting the chill of winter by staying under our quilt and joining in a time of prayer.

We grew very close. And Jesus was close also, because life's arena was so much smaller. I wasn't running to the office, then the hospital, then a church meeting, barely aware of His Presence. He seemed to come to us in the stillness.

Why not try to shrink your world a bit? You'll find more room for Him, and others.

—SCOTT HARRISON

PRAY: *Father, it seems like there is always either too much or too little of everything . . . space, responsibilities, time. Help us find more of You in every situation.*

DO: Shrink your life's arena if it will press you closer to God.

WHEN TRAGEDY STRIKES

◄◦►

READ: *Love . . . . always protects, always trusts, always hopes, always perseveres.*

—1 CORINTHIANS 13:6–7 (NIV)

REFLECT: When my mother suffered a stroke, my father insisted on taking care of her at home. For six years, until her death, he cared for her, waiting on her hand and foot, cooking, cleaning and doing all that was needed for her comfort. But most of all he loved her, and the love showed.

Watching this love in action, I saw my father in a new light. A new respect for him surged in me, and my own love increased. I became fully aware of what a blessing it is to have a father like mine. The joy of that discovery compensated for the sadness I felt for Mom, and it united our family in a stronger bond.

St. Paul said, "All things work together for good to them that love God . . ." (Romans 8:28). Both my parents loved God, and because of their love even tragedy was turned into good.   —BETTY RUTH GRAHAM

PRAY: *I believe Your promises, Lord—even the one that says something good will come out of tragedy.*

DO: Look back on a previous tragedy and make a list of good things that came out of it.

WHEN WORRY KEEPS YOU FROM WORKING

———————————◄○►———————————

READ: *"Be strong, all you people . . . and work; for I am with you," says the Lord. . . .*

—HAGGAI 2:4

REFLECT: It was already after noon, and I hadn't been able to sit still and focus for more than fifteen minutes. How would I ever get in a good day's work with all there was to fret about? First I worried about the world situation: Was anyone safe anymore? Then I turned to finances; I needed that tax refund this year more than ever. That reminded me of a health insurance claim I needed to fill out. I sorted through some papers, talked on the phone awhile and finally took a walk around the block.

The exercise helped a little. Back inside, I opened my Bible and turned to the short book of Haggai. Hadn't I marked a verse once for a day just like today? Something to help settle my thoughts so I could work:

"Work. For I am with you."

That did the trick.

—EVELYN BENCE

PRAY: *Lord, Your very presence settles me.*

DO: Write Haggai 2:4 on a piece of paper or index card and put it where you can read it often today.

WHEN YOU ARE AFRAID

---◄○►---

READ: *Comprehend with all the saints what is the width and length and depth and height to know the love of Christ which passes knowledge; that you may be filled with all the fullness of God.*

—EPHESIANS 3:17–19

REFLECT: Jesus fell on His knees, weeping and praying in the Garden of Gethsemane. He was alone, separated from His beloved disciples, and He needed to make a confession to His heavenly Father. He was afraid. In His divine power, He knew exactly what His future held—an agonizing death on the Cross. In His humanness He feared that future, and He confided that fear.

These dramatic moments at Gethsemane tell me two things. Even when God doesn't choose to change the circumstances, He sends an angel and the strength for us to cope. And secondly, prayer prepares us for our challenges. Jesus' doubts became determination through the process of prayer. You and I have the same source of power available to us!

—CAROL KUYKENDALL

PRAY: *Father, please use my prayers to turn my doubts into determination.*

DO: Confess your fear to God and meditate on Christ's fear as He faced the cross.

WHEN YOU ARE AFRAID ABOUT THE OUTCOME OF A PROJECT

<o>

READ: *"You shall know the truth, and the truth shall make you free."*

—JOHN 8:32

REFLECT: I've been afraid about many things as far back as I can remember—even after I became a Christian and asked God to fill me with His Spirit.

For example, one morning I was finishing a book project. I woke up afraid about it. I prayed that God would remove the fear. But He didn't. In fact, it got worse. So I practically redid the whole thing. When I still felt uneasy, I remembered that Dr. Paul Tournier had once said that fear is sometimes a message from God telling us to listen and find the meaning of it so we can grow spiritually.

So I asked myself, "What am I afraid will happen when this book comes out?" And the answer came almost at once: I'm being very open about my imperfections, and I'm afraid that some Christians may reject me.

Although I still felt the fear, I decided that I would rather be rejected by some than not try to help people in pain. I surrendered the outcome to God.

—KEITH MILLER

PRAY: *Lord, thank You that courage is not dependent on our getting rid of all our fear, but on offering it to You and trusting You.*

DO: Ask God the root of your fear and listen for His truth that will set you free.

WHEN YOU ARE DOUBTING YOUR VALUE

<o>

READ: *He chose us in Him before the foundation of the world, that we should be holy and without blame before Him in love. . . .*

—EPHESIANS 1:4

REFLECT: I sit outside in a rocker, listening to the melody of the tinkling wind chimes. I need this quiet time. A feeling of doubt has wound its way in and through me like a climbing vine. I find myself asking, *What is so special about me? Am I really able to offer God something that no one else has?*

I squint my eyes and search the blue expanse above me. A gust of wind sets the chimes to tinkling again. That's when I notice the different shapes and sizes of the metal cylinders. Each one, when moved by the wind, creates a different tone from the others.

In the tinkling of the wind chimes I seem to hear God saying, *No one else can create your expression of Me. You are needed to complete My song.* Those thoughts pull me free of the vine that has been choking me. No one else can create my expression of God!

—TERRY HELWIG

PRAY: *Thank You, Father, for the uniqueness of me . . . and all Your children.*

DO: Hang chimes outside a window. Let their song remind you that God's song isn't complete without you.

WHEN YOU ARE
FACING A CRISIS

—◄○►—

READ: *As we have opportunity, let us do good to all,*
especially to those who are of the household of faith.

—GALATIANS 6:10

REFLECT: I read somewhere that the Chinese word for crisis includes the symbol for opportunity. I know there are times when it is humanly impossible to see good in a crisis. Yet I can look back in my life and affirm that, indeed, crisis often brings opportunity.

I remember when my daughter Mandy was quite sick. I canceled meetings, delegated responsibilities and postponed many plans. Yet, of all the weeks I ever spent with Mandy, that was perhaps one of our best bonding times. Hours of reading books, rocking, slurping chicken noodle soup and even napping together left a very sweet experience in both our memories.

I think it's easier to look back and see the opportunities that crisis brings. But how would I be different if I looked for them in the present? I might be less fearful. I might be calmer, more open and, maybe, more creative.

—TERRY HELWIG

PRAY: *Father, help me see this crisis for what it is. And*
protect my imagination from imagining what it isn't.

DO: Give no place to fear in your crisis and look for the good God might bring from it.

WHEN YOU ARE
FEELING DOWN

—◄◦►—

READ: *To the end that my glory may sing praise to You and not be silent.*

—PSALM 30:12

REFLECT: It was late one Saturday before I found time to do laundry, and I was hurrying down the steps, tired and weary. Somehow I tripped. Clothes scattered and I found myself on my knees. There I blinked up at the most magnificent crimson sunset I had ever seen! My breath caught, and I forgot my awkward position.

"Oh, Father," I whispered, "How lovely! Thank You."

After a moment I picked myself up and continued toward the laundry room, but somehow the world around me looked different. An unexpected picture flashed into my mind. I could see my grandmother bending over her old washboard, tediously scrubbing clothes against its rough surface. *I'm so lucky*, I thought as I put my clothes into the automatic washer. *Thank You, God.* That day I learned a sure remedy for sadness: Look for just one thing to be grateful for, and thank God for it.

—DORIS HAASE

PRAY: *Magnificent Father, thank You for the displays of Your splendor all around us.*

DO: Practice replacing every trace of sadness with gratitude, for what God does and for Who He is.

WHEN YOU ARE
IN SITUATIONS
YOU CAN'T CONTROL

‹○›

READ: *All Your waves and billows have gone over me.*

—PSALM 42:7

REFLECT: The most annoying thing happened at our apartment in New York City. The neighbors upstairs began to remodel, moving walls and changing electrical and plumbing systems. All this activity caused a shower of dust to sift down into our apartment. Water leaked and ran down our walls, creating a real mess. Nothing could be done to stop the dust and disarray. For the first few weeks, I washed, mopped and dusted until I was exhausted.

At last, I realized my efforts were ridiculous. I needed to wait for the activity to end and then I could clean once and for all.

Sometimes difficulties in life come in repeated waves too. The important thing is not to struggle too hard against something I cannot change, but to hold on until the trouble passes. I know that it is in the trials of life that God can do His most important work in our souls.

—RUTH STAFFORD PEALE

PRAY: *When I'm in circumstances I can't change, Lord, help me to wait patiently until there is something productive I can do.*

DO: Stop striving. Wait for the right time to act.

WHEN YOU CAN'T
FORGIVE AND FORGET

◄O►

READ: *I, even I, am He who blots out your transgressions for My own sake; And I will not remember your sins.*

—ISAIAH 43:25

REFLECT: "I know John has told me he's sorry but it still bugs me," I said to my golfing partner.

"You don't believe in forgiveness?" Tim questioned.

"Sure I do. I've tried to forgive him and forget about it. But still, he lost my class notes." I sighed, took a few practice swings and hit a beautiful shot to within six feet of the hole. "Wow!" I exclaimed. "Sure is a lot better than dropping it in the water like I did on the last hole. This is one reason I like golf—every hole is a fresh chance. Guess that makes golf a lot like life."

I looked down the fairway at my ball, then back at the pond. "Hey, Tim, remind me to call John," I said, smiling. "I think it's time he and I move on to the next hole."

—JEFF JAPINGA

PRAY: *Father, I need Your Spirit to help me forget sins against me the way You forget mine against You.*

DO: Put a golf ball on your desk for a while to remind you to forgive and move on.

WHEN YOU CAN'T HEAR GOD SPEAKING

<del>◄◦►</del>

READ: *I will hear what God the Lord will speak.*

—PSALM 85:8

REFLECT: The woman at the next table was obviously expecting someone, whirling around each time the door to the coffee shop opened. At last her friend Ethel joined her.

Soon, everyone around was learning about the woman's problems. Clearly, she had more of them than anyone could be expected to handle alone. An alcoholic husband, a delinquent son, a diabetic condition. . . .

I found myself covertly studying Ethel's face. Warm, responsive, intelligent. I listened for the wisdom I was confident Ethel would supply.

"I wonder, Sue," she began, "if you've thought about—"

But Sue had launched into another melancholy story of failed help. I could almost see Ethel give up the effort to communicate. As I rose to leave I heard Sue's distressed voice: "I just wish I knew what to do!"

I thought of my words to God this very morning. "Why don't you give me an answer!"

Maybe, I thought, *He's been trying.*

—ELIZABETH SHERRILL

PRAY: *I find it hard, Lord, to keep silent long enough to hear You speak. Please help me to keep quiet so I can hear You.*

DO: Ask a friend to be honest enough to tell you when you're talking more than listening.

WHEN YOU CAN'T SEEM TO GET THE JOB DONE

―◄◦►―

READ: *Whoever does not receive the kingdom of God as a little child will by no means enter it.*

―MARK 10:15

REFLECT: Frustrated, I crawled out from under the bathroom sink where I was trying to replace a faucet pipe. "Honey," I yelled to my wife, "I just can't loosen these locknuts."

As I sat there, Joshua, our four-year-old, who was "helping," stood up, looked me in the eye and said, "Yes you can, Daddy. I *know* you can do it because you fixed the bricks by the front door!"

So I tackled the stubborn locknuts again, and thought about Josh's unwavering faith in his father.

Why can't I regain that kind of trust and faith? After all, didn't Jesus say that in order to enter His Kingdom we had to be like a little child?

Not only did the nuts eventually loosen and come off, but so did some of the grown-up pessimism I had acquired during my adult years.

―DOUG MEDUNA

PRAY: *Father, would You help daddies who are doubting their abilities today?*

DO: Refresh your optimism by asking a child to tell you what he/she knows about Jesus.

WHEN YOU CAN'T UNDERSTAND WHY

———◄o►———

READ: *In everything give thanks....*

— 1 THESSALONIANS 5:18

REFLECT: Someone once said that the most used word in Heaven for the first thousand years is going to be *Oh!*

Oh! That's why that happened! ... That's why You didn't allow us to go back to Oklahoma to practice pediatrics. You knew that we would be eternally grateful for the privilege of living and working in Waco, Texas, and raising our four children in a small university town.

Oh! Now I understand ... I had to go through a major depression to become sympathetic and helpful to friends.

Oh! That's what You were doing ... I fought so hard against enlarging our den, yet You knew that for the next twenty-five years we would need a large space for young college students who would come after church on Sunday nights for fellowship.

Oh! Thank You, Lord.

— DOROTHY SHELLENBERGER

PRAY: *Oh! Now I understand, Father. You don't think it's always necessary for me to know why certain things happen in my life.*

DO: Give up your "right" to always understand the why behind God's plans for you.

———

WHEN YOU DISLIKE SOMEONE

◄○►

READ: *He has made everything beautiful in its time.*

—ECCLESIASTES 3:11

REFLECT: A newcomer once joined our Sunday school class. I found her personality unpleasant and abrasive, and I was all set to ignore her when I suddenly remembered how my former art teacher once rescued a painting I had discarded. She placed it on something called a "finder"—two ninety-degree angles cut from mat board. By moving those pieces of framing around so they enclosed different portions of the painting, she finally located a section that held together as a lovely composition. Then she cut that section out, framed it and hung it on the wall.

I began to study the personality of my new classmate with a mental "finder," enclosing one quality at a time. And I made some remarkable discoveries! Courage. Honesty. Openness. Qualities that led to respect and eventually to friendship.

It's amazing how my negative attitudes change when I block out the troublesome areas and "frame" the beautiful aspects of another person. —MADGE HARRAH

PRAY: *God, thank You for seeing past the ugly to the beauty in me.*

DO: Hold a mental "finder" up to someone you think is unlikable. Compliment that person on a good quality that you see in him/her.

WHEN YOU DON'T FEEL
LIKE SMILING

◄○►

READ: *A merry heart does good, like medicine. . . .*

—PROVERBS 17:22

REFLECT: As I waited to see my doctor, I angrily leafed through a tattered magazine. One item described a scientific study on the physiological effects of smiling. It seems the act of smiling releases certain chemicals in the brain that act as natural mood elevators and painkillers, regardless of whether the smile was spontaneous or forced!

Could a smile, even a forced one, really improve my mood? It couldn't hurt to try, I decided.

I caught the eye of another patient and deliberately smiled as broadly as I could. She looked surprised, but smiled back. I held up the magazine and told her, "It says here that smiling makes us feel better—whether we have a reason to smile or not. What do you think?"

She paused, then laughed. "Now that you mention it, I think I do feel a little better."

I had to admit, so did I.

—SUSAN WILLIAMS

PRAY: *I pray for people who don't feel like smiling today. I'm one of them, Lord. Bring a smile to our faces, please.*

DO: Force yourself to smile at three people today and tell them why you're smiling.

WHEN YOU DON'T FEEL LOVING

------------◄○►------------

READ: *And now abide faith, hope, love, these three; but the greatest of these is love.*

—1 CORINTHIANS 13:13

REFLECT: Margot Pickett, the feminine half of the husband-and-wife team that ministers to our church, once had a novel suggestion. "Take the verses in I Corinthians 13:4–8," she advised, "and for the word *love*, substitute your name."

Then she followed with an example: "Margot suffers long and is kind," she read (albeit somewhat self-consciously). "Margot doesn't envy. Margot is not puffed up. Margot thinks no evil. Margot is not easily provoked. Margot bears all things, believes all things. Margot never fails."

She concluded the sermon with the suggestion that such an exercise might show us where we fall short of St. Paul's standard.

Those majestic verses certainly give us a goal to aim at, and they inspire us to strive ever harder for Christlike motives.

—FRED BAUER

PRAY: *Father God, You are the greatest of all.*

DO: Fill in your name for the word *love* in 1 Corinthians 13: 4–8.

WHEN YOU DON'T KNOW
HOW TO PRAY

—————————————◂◦▸—————————————

READ: *Now to Him who is able to do exceedingly abundantly above all that we ask or think, according to the power that works in us. . . .*

—EPHESIANS 3:20

REFLECT: Scripture gives us many pictures of God, and I find that when I cannot pray with words, I can pray through pictures.

When a friend is critically ill and I do not know whether to ask for healing or release from pain, I picture myself simply lifting my friend to the throne of grace and into the presence of God (Hebrews 4:16).

When I am baffled by my own circumstances or feelings, I picture myself creeping into my heavenly Father's lap, gratefully aware that "the eternal God is your refuge, And underneath are the everlasting arms . . ." (Deuteronomy 33:27).

When I am tempted, I recall that "we are surrounded by . . . a cloud of witnesses" (Hebrews 12:1) and picture beloved friends who are now with God, bending down from heaven to encourage me.

If words won't come, don't let that stop your prayers. God's gift of imagination can also be a doorway to prayer.

—PATRICIA HOUCK SPRINKLE

PRAY: *Father, receive my feelings and thoughts as prayers of faith.*

DO: Take your creative prayers a step further—write, draw or sing them.

WHEN YOU DON'T KNOW
WHAT LIES AHEAD

---◄◎►---

READ: *This is the day the Lord has made; We will rejoice and be glad in it.*

—PSALM 118:24

REFLECT: As a child when I visited my uncle and aunt on their farm, I found that they arose while it was still very dark. At breakfast, before going out into the fields, my uncle always prayed, thanking the Lord for the beautiful day. Of course it was much too dark for us to see the kind of day that was dawning.

One morning I said to my uncle, "Yesterday you thanked the Lord for a beautiful day, and it rained all day."

"Yep," he said, "and what a beautiful rain it was!"

Now I realize that my uncle's prayer was the kind that the Lord cherishes most—thanks for what we don't even know awaits us.   —FAYE FIELD

PRAY: *Thank You, Lord, for this beautiful day. Even if it's storming outside, I choose to be grateful for what this day holds.*

DO: Get up before dark, thank God for the beautiful day ahead and then see what the day brings.

WHEN YOU DON'T
LIKE YOURSELF

◄○►

READ: *Every good gift and every perfect gift is from above. . . .*

—JAMES 1:17

REFLECT: I had driven the carpool that day and my nine-year-old grandson had left a sheet of paper graded with an A. On it, he had printed boldly: I help others, I'm caring, I'm kind, I'm talented, I share. . . .

Hmmm, he has a high opinion of himself, I thought. It bothered me enough that I asked his teacher about it.

"An excellent paper," she said. "Bo has a fine self-image."

"Isn't it a little conceited?" I asked.

"The assignment was to list things for which to give thanks. Most of the children listed material possessions. Bo had a different idea." She smiled, turning the paper over.

On the back he had written: "Thank You, Lord, for me and my talents. I love You dearly. Amen." It was signed with a red heart trailing a rainbow tail.

—ELAINE ST. JOHNS

PRAY: *Father, thank You for the pleasure You get out of the gifts and talents You've placed in each of us. Help us to recognize and appreciate them too, in ourselves as well as others.*

DO: Write God a thank-you note for you and your talents, signed with a red heart trailing a rainbow tail.

WHEN YOU DOUBT
YOU'RE UP TO A TASK

◄○►

READ: *By my God I can leap over a wall.*

—PSALM 18:29

REFLECT: At a flea market I came across an early edition of *The Little Engine That Could.* "Hannah," I called to our seven-year-old granddaughter. "Come. I want to read you an important story." She came running.

I read the story with enthusiasm and sound effects. Hannah seemed hypnotized.

At last I closed the book. "Well, Hannah, the next time you face a problem that's a mountain to you, what are you going to say?"

She shrugged and said, "I'll say, 'Oh, brother, here we go again.'"

I suppose all of us have ambivalent feelings before a difficult task. "I think I can—I think I can't—I think I can. . . ."

No, I can't do everything I think I can. I once tried to water-ski, and all I got for my trouble was a hernia. But whether I'm facing my first public speech or chemotherapy, a good first step is for me to say, "With God's help, I can do this."

—DANIEL SCHANTZ

PRAY: *God, help me believe in myself and Your enabling power.*

DO: Read or reread *The Little Engine That Could.*

WHEN YOU ENCOUNTER PREJUDICE

---◄○►---

READ: *The Lord had said unto Abram . . . I will bless them that bless thee . . . and in thee shall all families of the earth be blessed.*

—GENESIS 12:1–3

REFLECT: When Keith and I arrived at the monastery for a visit one year, Mother Hildegard met us at the gate and said, "I have to warn you. My mother is visiting, and she's always been very prejudiced against Jews."

Keith and I looked at each other and shrugged, "Look, we can't be other than we are," I said to her. "We'll deal with it."

During the week of our stay, we acted no differently than usual. We tease each other a lot, so we laugh a lot. We were friendly toward the other guests, helped them, answered their questions, worked alongside them.

We left before Mother Hildegard's mother did. When I called later to find out how things were going, she said, "Well, you'll never guess what! Since you've been gone, my mother's been moping around, and when I asked her what was wrong, she said, 'I miss my little Jewish couple!'"

—RHODA BLECKER

PRAY: *Lord, no matter what our differences are, let us bless You by loving each other.*

DO: Open your heart and reach out to someone who is different from you.

WHEN YOU FEAR
BEING ALONE

READ: *"I will never leave you nor forsake you."*

—HEBREWS 13:5

REFLECT: When my neighbors received word of a family emergency, I offered to stay with their three-year-old Amy for a few days.

We looked through picture books, baked cookies, repaired a teddy bear's ear. . . . By nightfall I was so tired that I couldn't wait to go to bed.

But Amy couldn't fall asleep. Could she have a glass of water? Another blanket? A doll? I was losing patience. "Amy," I said, "it's time to go to sleep!"

She looked up at me, her wide eyes filled with concern. "You won't go away, will you?" she asked.

Then I understood. Amy was afraid she might wake to find herself alone.

Hugging her close, I promised, "Honey, I'm going to be here every minute . . . even when you're sound asleep."

I thought of my own childlike fear of being left alone. And I thanked God for His love that constantly reassures me that He is always there.

—PHYLLIS HOBE

PRAY: *Sometimes, God, I feel alone even when I'm not alone. Thank You for being with me in those times and always.*

DO: Keep something close to represent God's nearness when you're alone—maybe a teddy bear or your favorite children's book.

WHEN YOU FEEL
A SENSE OF URGENCY

◄○►

READ: *It was not you who sent me here, but God. . . .*

—GENESIS 45:8

REFLECT: "I'd been picking the wild grapes along the veranda, but before I made jelly I thought I'd stretch out on the sofa for a nap," my elderly mother explained on the phone. I could just see her, slippers kicked off, glasses folded on the paper stand.

"I don't know how long I slept, but when I really woke up I was halfway across the street on my way to Helen's." Helen was another senior who had lived alone since her husband was hospitalized. "I was wearing my slippers and apron. I thought maybe I should go back and change, but something told me I was needed."

Just as they were about to enjoy a cup of tea, Helen's phone rang. "Hello? Yes, this is Helen. No, I'm not alone. A neighbor just dropped by unexpectedly."

Helen suddenly sat down, her face ashen. She looked at Mom with tear-filled eyes. "That was the hospital. My husband just passed away."

Suddenly Mom knew why she had come and Who had urged her on.

—ALMA BARKMAN

PRAY: *Father, please lead me to a neighbor who needs a friend.*

DO: Trust God to send you where, and when, you're needed.

WHEN YOU FEEL ABANDONED

―◁○▷―

READ: *Suddenly a great tempest arose on the sea, so that the boat was covered with the waves. But He was asleep.*

—MATTHEW 8:24

REFLECT: I remember the gentle touch of my grandfather's hands on my ankles, when I was two or three, as he coaxed me out from under a bed during a thunderstorm. He sat me on his lap on the porch outside and explained how the big clouds bang into each other and yell, "Ow!" Grandpa exulted in the fury of the skies. Soon I, too, caught his excitement and lost my fear.

Emotional storms have not been so easily resolved. Like His disciples, I tend to ask God, "Don't You care?" At least I did until Pastor Sam came to our church. "Has it ever occurred to you," he asked about Jesus sleeping in the storm-tossed boat, "how He slept, safe, unafraid, with those He loved?"

No, it had never occurred to me.

"He does us the same honor," said Pastor Sam.

And so now, when life's storms overtake me, instead of "waking up Jesus" with the same old accusations, I feel a sense of honor, not abandonment. —BRENDA WILBEE

PRAY: *Lord Jesus, let me always sleep safe, unafraid because You're in my boat.*

DO: Be a peaceful influence in the midst of a friend's storm.

When you feel defeated

<o>

READ: *The Spirit also helps in our weaknesses.*

—ROMANS 8:26

REFLECT: Among the participants in a study about identical twins were a pair of twin brothers in their forties whose lives were quite opposite. One was a happily married lawyer with a flourishing practice; the other, a twice-divorced alcoholic who had gone from job to job all his life. The questionnaire they filled out asked, "What made you the way you are?" The researchers were amazed that these two men had written identical answers to that question, "My father's death when I was ten years old."

Clearly, it's not what happens to us that makes us happy people or unhappy people. It's how we *react* to what happens. If there's a lot of stress in my life, I can let it make me sick or I can use it to get stronger. My weakness can defeat me, or it can make me wonderfully aware of God's strength!

—MARILYN MORGAN KING

PRAY: *Almighty God, help my weakness make me more secure and happier because it makes me wonderfully aware of Your strength.*

DO: Try to choose to be happy today, even in—no, especially in—your struggle and weakness.

WHEN YOU FEEL GUILTY

READ: *Create in me a clean heart, O God, And renew a steadfast spirit within me.*

—PSALM 51:10

REFLECT: I was sixteen. Mom had accepted my offer to run an errand, and my visiting uncle had entrusted me with his Chevy. As the car left our driveway, I heard a scraping sound and glimpsed the wiggling of our iron post mailbox. "Nothing happened," I told myself hopefully.

Later, I went through the motions of eating dinner and waving good-bye to Uncle Ing and Aunt Helen. Then I slipped up to my bedroom. Occasionally, I looked out my window to watch my father watering the grass. Finally, I made my way outdoors and blurted out everything.

"I'm sure I scratched the car door."

"No, you didn't," my father replied.

"I didn't? How do you know?" I asked.

"I saw the mailbox sway as you drove away. When you returned, I took a look."

"Dad," I wondered out loud, "why didn't you tell me?"

My father looked at me and simply said, "I wanted you to come to me."

—STEPHANIE LINDSELL

PRAY: *Thank You, God, for the joy of an unburdened heart!*

DO: If you have something weighing on you today, set yourself free by confessing it to the appropriate person.

WHEN YOU FEEL INFERIOR

---◄◦►---

READ: *He chose the lowly things of this world....*

— 1 CORINTHIANS 1:28 (NIV)

REFLECT: "Hey, it fits good!" said five-year-old Geoffrey from inside the floppy tent of his older brother's sweatshirt.

When he heard me laugh, Geoffrey poked his head out and said, "I'm not too little!" Then he stormed upstairs and slammed his door.

Later, I peeked in to find both boys sprawled on the bed.

"You're big enough," Tim was saying. "You're just right for five years old."

You're just right.... For a year, I had tried to model myself after a woman I admired: a well-known Christian church woman, mother and wife. Gradually it dawned on me that I hadn't even come close to emulating the woman I admired. I wasn't her size! Nevertheless, I had grown in essential areas like reading the Bible regularly and praying.

Sometimes the desire to grow makes us feel "too little," when in reality we are just the right size for now—and always good enough in God's eyes. —LINDA CHING SLEDGE

PRAY: *Lord, I need to see myself as You see me and want me to be.*

DO: Ask God how He sees you, for now, and who you are becoming.

WHEN YOU FEEL
LIKE A LOSER

<o>

READ: *Though I walk through the valley of the shadow of death, I will fear no evil, for You are with me.*

—PSALM 23:4

REFLECT: In the last seconds of our semifinal game, the basketball team I coached had gone from being one point ahead to losing by one point—from screaming excitement to tears of disappointment.

I called the team together and said, "Boys, losing doesn't make you losers. Only acting beaten can make you a loser."

Nobody burst into a cheer, but the tears dried up. Then the youngest player said, "Mr. Fellman, are you going to come back and coach next year?"

"Sure, Neal," I replied.

"Great!" said Neal.

It meant a lot to the boys that I was there for the winning and the losing. I guess that's why God makes so many promises to be with us in "the valley of the shadow of death" or "to the very end of the world." He knows that life has many losses and He plans to be there. Our "Coach" never quits on us.

—ERIC FELLMAN

PRAY: *Jesus, thank You for Your death on the cross, the world's greatest victory out of what looked like the greatest loss.*

DO: Separate your identity from your loss. Don't let it define you.

WHEN YOU FEEL LIKE COMPLAINING

‹◦›

READ: *Hear the instruction of your father, And do not forsake the law of your mother. . . .*

—PROVERBS 1:8

REFLECT: There's a huge pothole in the red mud in front of us. Our Jeep has been climbing painfully up into the Tanzanian mountains. The whole family is thirsty and shaken up. I open my mouth to complain and then shut it again.

The voice of my late mother comes into my head. "Count your blessings, my dear." Without hesitation, I begin to count:

One, I am visiting this breathtaking country with my grown-up children, who are traveling with their parents of their own free will.

Two, I live in a country of surfaced roads and indoor plumbing.

Three, I had the kind of mother whose words of wisdom have stayed with me after she herself was gone.

We maneuvered around the pothole and reached the top of the hill, and I was still counting my blessings.

—BRIGITTE WEEKS

PRAY: *Thank You, Father, for a wise mother whose words still correct and guide me.*

DO: Name your blessings until you can't think of any more to name.

When you feel like giving up

———————◄◊►———————

READ: *Uphold me according to Your word, that I may live; And do not let me be ashamed of my hope.*

—PSALM 119:116

REFLECT: When Dad was a youngster he began his sailing career racing Snowbirds in Southern California, competing with a class of older and far more experienced sailors. His first summer, Dad finished last in every race, sometimes even after the race committee boat had gone, sometimes when no one was there to log him in. But he finished, and his persistence did not go unnoticed. At the end of the season at the awards banquet, an elderly lady who had watched all the races from her front porch called him forward to present a special trophy, "The Hope Cup," she called it, because no matter how discouraged Dad might have been, he never gave up hope.

That battered cup has become a perpetual trophy in my family as it's passed from member to member. It reminds me to stick with the task, no matter what.

—RICK HAMLIN

PRAY: *Forgive me, Lord, for giving up too easily. Please hang in here with me as long as it takes to cross the finish line.*

DO: Find a friend who will stay in the race with you, encouraging you until the end.

When you feel lost

READ: *I will say of the Lord, "He is my refuge and my fortress; My God, in Him I will trust."*

—PSALM 91:2

REFLECT: Sam was my best dog ever, a field trial dog who found birds and pointed them with contagious enthusiasm. He was much more than a bird dog, though. Often we'd share lazy lunches and a snooze in an abandoned apple orchard.

One afternoon, Sam and I became separated. I called and whistled. No sign of him. I had to get back to town for an important appointment, but how could I leave Sam?

Then I remembered a trick. I laid my shirt on the ground under the branches of a bush.

I worried all night. But when I returned the next morning, there was Sam curled up with his nose under the sleeve of my shirt.

Later I wondered. When I get lost, do I look for some part of God's Word, curl up in it and wait patiently, knowing that my Friend will find me if I just have faith in Him?

—SCOTT HARRISON

PRAY: *Thank You, Father, for the comfort of Your Word. And thank You that I can always find You there.*

DO: Look for a Scripture to wrap yourself in today.

WHEN YOU FEEL
NEGLECTED AND ALONE

—◇—

READ: *Ask, and it will be given to you; seek, and you will find; knock, and it will be opened to you.*

—MATTHEW 7:7

REFLECT: Worried about intruders, my friend Marcy kept her door locked all day. She had to remember to unlock it each afternoon before her first-grade daughter Sharon came home from school. One afternoon I was visiting, and we were so engrossed in our conversation that she forgot to unlock the door at 3:00 PM. At 3:15 she suddenly jumped up, aware that Sharon had not come in. When she opened the door Sharon was sitting on the front step, sobbing. "Oh, honey, I'm sorry," Marcy said, gathering the little girl in her arms. "But why didn't you knock? We were here all the time."

Have there been times you've felt neglected and alone? No matter how alone you may feel, you have only to knock and God will open the door to comfort and console you.

—BETTY R. GRAHAM

PRAY: *Many times, all I've needed to do is knock and enter into Your presence and, still, I waited outside alone and hurting. I'm so grateful You're always available, Father.*

DO: When you feel alone and left out, go to a special room in your house and meet with God.

WHEN YOU FEEL OVERWHELMED

READ: *Then the waters would have overwhelmed us,*
The stream would have gone over our soul. . . .

—PSALM 124:4

REFLECT: I'm in the midst of what I call "convergence," a kind of storm of stressful things all happening at once.

My wife and I have been building a new home. Nothing I have done in all my sixty-one years has tested my patience like working with contractors, discontinued products and hundreds of on-the-spot decisions. Meanwhile, I'm trying to meet deadlines and prepare for school, which starts in fourteen days. And today the phone rang with the worst news of all: My father has only a few days to live.

I don't think there's any conspiracy about these storms. They happen for the same reason that everyone comes to the checkout stand at the same time—they just do.

No one escapes these storms of convergence, but the Psalmist reminds me that, "Blessed be the Lord, Who has not given us as prey to their teeth." And, "Our help is in the name of the Lord, Who made heaven and earth" (Psalm 124:6–8).

I'm counting on that.

—DANIEL SCHANTZ

PRAY: *I'm sorry, Lord. I'm so distracted I can't pray a sensible prayer, so I turn this chaos over to You.*

DO: Don't think about your problem; think about God, your solution.

WHEN YOU FEEL THREATENED

<hr>

READ: *Let us fix our eyes on Jesus, the author and perfecter of our faith, who for the joy set before him endured the cross, scorning its shame, and sat down at the right hand of the throne of God.*

—HEBREWS 12:2 (NIV)

REFLECT: In one of my Bibles is a picture of Daniel in the lion's den. What I like most is the position Daniel has taken. He has turned his back on the lion, with his hands bound behind his back. Daniel is looking up toward a small window, praying. He is looking at his source of strength instead of the menacing problem.

I like to study the crouching lion too. One day it occurred to me that he had a baffled expression on his giant face. He wasn't accustomed to coming up against fearless men. Confused, maybe even fearful himself, he sat there and did nothing. Daniel walked out of the den without a scratch.

Sooner or later all of us find ourselves in a lion's den. Like Daniel, look up to God, Who is bigger and stronger than any enemy in the world. Turn your back on your fearful problem and face a God Who is waiting to hear from you.

—MADGE HARRAH

PRAY: *Almighty God, help me to have faith that can turn my back to my enemy and look to You, my source of strength.*

DO: Focus on God and what He is able to do, not your problem.

<hr>

WHEN YOU FEEL UNLOVING AND UNLOVED

◄○►

READ: *Understanding is a wellspring of life to him who has it.*

—PROVERBS 16:22

REFLECT: When my mother-in-law phoned us one evening to tell us about her new dog, I was surprised. "Another dog?" I said to my wife Carol. "She already has three . . . and now Missouri the Pug?"

But when we visited at my in-laws' home a week later and were greeted by this puppy wagging his tail so hard he almost fell over, licking our faces, his eyes shining with friendliness and trust, I soon relented.

"Mo" and I became great pals—going for walks, playing catch, shaking hands. But I'm especially grateful to Missouri for a very simple lesson he taught me. If ever I am uneasy about meeting strangers, I think of our first meeting. He didn't hesitate or hold back, waiting to see what I thought of him, if I wanted to be friends or not. No, he jumped right into my lap. He was instantly lovable because he instantly loved.

—RICK HAMLIN

PRAY: *God, I'm not going to jump on anyone's lap to make a friend, but I could definitely be a lot friendlier. Give me courage to be the first to reach out.*

DO: Make the first move toward friendship today. Smile before you're smiled at. Invite an acquaintance out for a cup of coffee before you're invited.

WHEN YOU FEEL UNPRODUCTIVE

READ: *It has not yet been revealed what we shall be....*

—1 JOHN 3:2

REFLECT: A man was going to give me a prize rosebush, but what he showed me appeared to be a dead stick with some dry strings attached to the bottom. Now, I know what a rose looks like and can recognize its beauty and fragrance, but I did not see these delightful things in this dry stick. But he assured me that if I planted the stick, in due time, God would perform the miracle of producing a thriving plant, covered with lovely fragrant prize roses. And it was true. In due time, the most beautiful, sweet-smelling roses I had ever seen appeared on the plant.

I was musing about the rosebush as I thought about my life—how some areas of it seem as unproductive and barren as that prize rosebush. But if God can make something that looks like a dry stick with strings thrive, I thought, then He can make those parts of me thrive too. —LEE WEBBER

PRAY: *I'm dying on the vine, Lord. Please breathe Your beauty and fragrance into my life.*

DO: Start with a seed of talent. Ask God to bless it and begin using it for His glory.

WHEN YOU FEEL UNQUALIFIED

◄◦►

READ: ... *Thoroughly equipped for every good work.*

—2 TIMOTHY 3:17

REFLECT: I used to be the world's champ when it came to feeling unqualified. I was forever thinking anyone could do a better job than I could—any job. But a number of years ago a good friend, who had raised four children, told me, "It's funny, when we're young and don't know the first thing about raising kids—we have them. We blunder along, trying to learn about life and kids at the same time. And somehow we can even get excited about it. I guess that just proves the old saying, 'The Lord doesn't call the qualified, He qualifies the called.'"

So now, when I get in one of my I-can't-because-I'm-unqualified moods, I tell myself that I can teach that Sunday school class, I can talk to the kids in the neighborhood about the Lord—not because I'm qualified, but because the Lord is with me.

—BRIAN MILLER

PRAY: *Forgive me, Lord, for making excuses for not serving. I can't say yes to everything, but I can say yes to You and what You want me to do.*

DO: Encourage an insecure friend not to be led by his/her insecurities.

WHEN YOU FEEL
YOU'RE SUFFERING ALONE

<>

READ: *For in that He Himself has suffered, being tempted, He is able to aid those who are tempted.*

—HEBREWS 2:18

REFLECT: When my son announced that he was going overseas as an aerial photographer for the U.S. Air Force during a time of international crisis, I was sick with worry about his safety. It was worry that I felt I had to endure alone because I thought no one else would understand.

Then came the day I was talking to my husband about my feelings of loneliness. "You just don't understand," I blurted out.

"You know better than that," he said gently as he took me in his arms. "Have you forgotten that I, too, served overseas during the war? Or that Bryce is my son too?"

Yes, I had forgotten—momentarily. I guess we all forget in the midst of our own suffering that others do understand. And those who understand most of all are those who have experienced sorrow, frustration, despair. Isn't that one reason why I feel so at ease with Jesus?

—JUNE MASTERS BACHER

PRAY: *Lord Jesus, no one has suffered as You have. Remind me of that when I feel no one understands my pain.*

DO: Hug a friend who is feeling fearful.

WHEN YOU FIND YOURSELF
JUDGING OTHERS

‹○›

READ: *"Inasmuch as you did it to one of the least of these My brethren, you did it to Me."*

—MATTHEW 25:40

REFLECT: My friend John took his three-year-old son Joey to a Frontier Days parade. The street was crowded, but they found the perfect viewing spot—almost. "Their" corner was also occupied by a scruffy, bearded young man. So while Joey watched the procession of marching bands and prancing horses and floats, John watched the man. Was he homeless? Would he ask for a handout or a place to stay? John didn't relax until the man shouldered his way past them and melted into the crowd. After the last cowboy rode into the sunset, Joey turned and asked, "Daddy, who was that man?" John was about to say, "Oh, just some bum," when Joey added, softly, "Daddy, do you think that man was Jesus?"

"I'd always considered myself a mature, caring Christian," John told me later, "but Joey brought me face to face with a private sin: my judgmental attitude toward people who aren't like me. It's hard work, but I'm trying to follow Joey's example and look for Jesus in everyone I meet."

—PENNEY SCHWAB

PRAY: *Precious Lord, change my way of seeing so that I can see You in everyone I meet.*

DO: Give a friend permission to remind you of your commitment not to judge people by their looks when they catch you doing it.

WHEN YOU HAVE A CHANCE TO DO A SECRET KINDNESS

READ: *Your Father who sees in secret will Himself reward you openly.*

—MATTHEW 6:4

REFLECT: I turned into our driveway and saw several sheets of wet paper littering the yard. If I didn't pick them up, I knew my husband Jim would when he came home. The temptation to leave the papers was strong.

Suddenly Ruth's name came to mind. When she babysat our daughter, mysterious little things happened at our house. The chrome on the stove might look shinier, or smudges might have disappeared from the kitchen window.

I asked Ruth if she ever cleaned things while I was gone. She did. She said she tried to do one nice thing secretly every single day.

With that memory still fresh, I climbed out of the car and picked up the papers. And when Jim came home from work? I just smiled and basked in the warmth that comes from doing secret kindnesses.

—TERRY HELWIG

PRAY: *Lord God, I'm so capable of not doing that secret kindness, of leaving it because I know someone else will do it. Forgive me, Lord. Help me to first think of doing the kind thing.*

DO: Remember that feeling of satisfaction the last time you did a little kindness.

WHEN YOU HAVE AN OPPORTUNITY TO HELP

◄○►

READ: *"Is it a small matter...?"*

—GENESIS 30:15

REFLECT: I had just gotten out of my car at the retirement home where I'd gone to visit a friend. A car pulled up behind me, and a lovely older lady got out. As I unloaded my car, I heard a scraping sound, like something being dragged across the pavement. I glanced over to see that she had dropped a small box and was pushing it with her foot across the parking lot.

"Can I help you with that?" I asked as I walked over to pick up the package. When I handed it—a set of new lipsticks—to her, she couldn't thank me enough.

"Oh, you're such a dear," she said. "With this hip I just can't bend over." She then insisted I take one of the lipsticks as thanks.

How very little effort it can take to help someone. It doesn't make a big difference, sure, but a small difference can make all the difference to the person with the need.

—GINA BRIDGEMAN

PRAY: *Father, help me recognize opportunities You give me to provide exactly what someone needs, no matter how small it may seem.*

DO: Be on the lookout daily for opportunities to help others.

WHEN YOU HAVE AN OPPORTUNITY TO SHARE YOUR FAITH

<o>

READ: *"I heard the voice of the Lord, saying: Whom shall I send and who will go for Us?"*

—ISAIAH 6:8

REFLECT: Just before I left for my new job, my wife Nicole said, "God gave you this job for a reason beyond work. Keep an eye out for why He brought you there."

The writer I was to replace spent a week training me. We became fast friends and I shared my faith with him. He said he was taking a four-month backpacking trip and was packed so full he had only about "this much space" left in his bag.

Well, "this much space" looked Bible-size to me. So I asked Nicole to pick up the smallest Bible she could find. Before he left, I put it on his desk.

Later, I received an e-mail from him. He was in a run-down old camper in New Zealand, reading the Bible by flashlight. He wrote, "I am reading with much interest. Thanks again."

God gives me many opportunities to serve. If I don't look for them, I wonder how many I'll miss.

—DAVE FRANCO

PRAY: *Lord, help me make the best of the space You give me to witness to You, even if it's only "this much."*

DO: Ask God why you are where you are today and who there has room for faith in his/her life.

WHEN YOU HAVE
FINANCIAL FEARS

‹○›

READ: *When he saw that the wind was boisterous, he was afraid; and beginning to sink he cried out, saying, "Lord, save me!"*

—MATTHEW 14:30

REFLECT: Henry A. Ironside, a minister, wrote, "What Peter should have remembered was that he could no more walk on smooth water than on rough waves, except by the power of the Lord, and that power is as great in the storm as in the calm."

One of my waves of fear is financial. I know God provides, but when the porch roof is leaking and my car's odometer is at two hundred thousand miles, I start to sink.

When Peter cried out to Jesus, the Lord pulled him up. "Why did you doubt?" He asked him. When my storms blow in, I cry out. And God lifts me up, whether it's with a new freelance opportunity, or the realization that a bike ride and a picnic can be as much fun as a movie and eating out.

His power is as great in the storm as in the calm. Why did I doubt?

—MARJORIE PARKER

PRAY: *God, I believe You are more than able for any need I could have. Help my unbelief.*

DO: Speak peace to the storms of fear and doubt raging inside you.

WHEN YOU HAVE
MONSTER-SIZE WORRIES

◄◦►

READ: *You broke the heads of Leviathan in pieces....*

—PSALM 74:14

REFLECT: My son Geoffrey had a love-hate relationship with monsters. I worried until I saw that he not only brought monsters to life in his mind, he conquered them.

He learned everything about one monster, read books and decorated his room with pictures of it. Then, when the monster was conjured up in all its fearsomeness, Geoffrey would climb into my lap and say, "I'm scared."

"Okay," I'd say. "Here's what we can do." We'd think of ways the monster could be banished, and say a prayer. "God, chase the monster out of my head."

Then Geoffrey would take down the pictures and return the books to the library. With my help, he'd tamed his monster—until the next one.

The system works for any monster-size worry.

—LINDA CHING SLEDGE

PRAY: *Jesus, I'm so grateful You've already conquered all things that frighten me.*

DO: Picture yourself leaving each of your worries, one by one, at the foot of the cross.

WHEN YOU HAVE
NO WORDS TO PRAY

————————◄o►————————

READ: *The Lord knows the thoughts of man.*

—PSALM 94:11

REFLECT: I once heard the story of Sam, a devout man who lived deep in the Appalachian hills of Tennessee. Sam had occasion in his comings and goings to pass by a little church nestled among the maples and oaks in the valley. Each time he would stop, walk softly down the aisle in his oversized work shoes and kneel at the altar. Being a man of few words, Sam would say, simply, "Lord, it's me, Sam." After which, so the story goes, he would remain kneeling in silence for several minutes, rise and leave, comfortable in the knowledge that God "knew what was layin' on my heart."

Now, when I am at a loss for words, when I feel unworthy of prayer, I think of Sam and I kneel and say, simply, "Lord, it's me, Mary Jane." Like Sam, I am comforted knowing that God "knows what's layin' on my heart."

—MARY JANE MEYER

PRAY: *Lord, it's me,* _____.

DO: Kneel in silence, confident that God knows what is "layin' on" your heart.

When you have
too much to do

◄○►

READ: *I must work the works of Him who sent Me while it is day; the night is coming when no one can work.*

—JOHN 9:4

REFLECT: It had been a hectic week. Rushing to complete my seminar notes, I glanced at my cocker spaniel Bucky furiously scratching at fleas. For more than a week I had intended to wash the pup, but something else always barked louder. Gathering my notes, I snapped a leash on Bucky's collar. Harried man and flea-bitten dog jumped into my Jeep and roared off down the road.

As I arranged with the veterinarian to have Bucky groomed, I noticed a sign tacked on her office wall: "God put me on earth to accomplish a certain number of things. Right now I'm so far behind I'll never die." My wide grin became rolling laughter. Life is indeed hectic. We never get "caught up." I'll never have the time to do all that I want to do, so I had better make wise choices.

I reviewed my three-page, single-spaced to do list and decided what must be accomplished, and what can wait—forever, perhaps.

—SCOTT WALKER

PRAY: *Father, make me wise to the things on my "to do" list that rob my time.*

DO: *Thin your "to do" list down to the essentials.*

WHEN YOU KNOW A WIDOW
WHO IS HURTING

◄○►

READ: *At midnight Paul and Silas were praying and singing hymns to God. . . .*

—ACTS 16:25

REFLECT: I'd been trying to tell my minister how alienated and alone I felt, how difficult it was to be widowed. He began to tell me the story of Paul and Silas in prison in Philippi.

I listened impatiently. What connection was there between my problem and this biblical account of Paul and Silas? Finally, annoyed that he had paid so little attention to my hurts, I said, "I'm afraid I don't get the connection."

"Don't you?" he asked. "Strange, but I would have said you've been describing a midnight hour of your life."

Ah, that! "And so I have," I answered.

"Well, Paul and Silas certainly were facing a midnight hour! And what does the Scripture tell us they were doing? Why, praying and singing hymns to God!" Pausing a moment, he looked directly at me and asked, "Ever thought of trying that?"

I hadn't, but I did. And it helps.

—NITA SCHUH

PRAY: *Holy Comforter, reach down and embrace widows everywhere who feel alienated and alone.*

DO: Copy this devotional and send it to a grieving widow.

WHEN YOU LACK FAITH

◄◦►

READ: *Let us therefore come boldly to the throne of grace, that we may obtain mercy and find grace to help in time of need.*

—HEBREWS 4:16

REFLECT: A friend of mine, paralyzed in an auto accident, needed my prayers, but I had no faith that she would recover. What good were prayers without faith? I felt I was letting her down until I remembered some advice my mother once gave me. In a crisis God has different roles for each to play.

The idea came to me that even if I lacked faith, there were many others who did not. I mailed requests to thirty friends, asking them to pray for God's best for my injured friend. I couldn't bring myself to ask them to pray for full recovery. I wrote her, suggesting she open herself up to God's power.

Seven months later came her thanks, with the news that soon she would return to work. I think that the next time a friend needs me, my role will be that of the prayer of faith.

—DEE ANN PALMER

PRAY: *I truly believe nothing is too difficult for You, Father, including giving me faith to believe in a friend's healing.*

DO: Send an e-mail gathering prayer support for a friend in need.

WHEN YOU LACK FINANCES TO MEET A NEED

READ: *Thanks be to God for his indescribable gift!*

—2 CORINTHIANS 9:15

REFLECT: As Parkinson's disease continued to devastate my husband Bob, we realized we would need an electric hospital bed at home. With other medical expenses taking a big chunk of our income, purchasing one seemed impossible.

"We can't give up," our daughter Emily said during a winter visit. "Let's all pray for a way to be open for him to have one."

One day in April a fellow employee in the insurance company where Emily works called her into her office. "This is Mrs. Walton," she told Emily. "I think you two have something in common. You need an electric hospital bed, and she has one to get rid of."

"How much are you asking for it?" Emily asked.

"I don't want to sell it," Mrs. Walton answered. "I want to give it to someone who can use it. It was my husband's, and since his death, I've been looking for someone to give it to."

Emily recognized the bed as a gift from God. I knew it was too.

—DRUE DUKE

PRAY: *I praise You, Almighty God, for Your amazing provision that tells me You're so aware of my needs.*

DO: Pass along something you no longer need that could be an answer to another's prayer.

WHEN YOU NEED A BREATH
OF FRESH AIR

―◆◯►―

READ: *When you pass through the waters, I will be with you. . . .*

―ISAIAH 43:2

REFLECT: Spiders have always fascinated me. As a child, I would marvel at the huge, crystalline webs that stretched between the rows in our cornfield—and at their hairy, yellow-and-black occupants. I read recently that one species of spider can stay under water for ten hours, breathing from an air bubble it takes along.

Sometimes I feel overwhelmed by the sorrows and trials I face. Loved ones are ill; friends disappoint me. I bungle a job interview or an apology or a new recipe. Problems and misunderstandings flood over me, and I find myself sinking beneath their weight.

But, like that special spider, I have an "air bubble" to provide me with what I need: God's Word. In reading His promises, I am comforted and upheld, buoyed by the reality of divine presence in the midst of daily predicaments.

And soon, with His help, I find myself on top of the water once again.

―MARY LOU CARNEY

PRAY: *I love Your Word, Father. It is life and breath to me.*

DO: Study a spider and give God glory for His amazing creation.

WHEN YOU NEED A FRIEND

READ: *A friend loves at all times....*

—PROVERBS 17:17

REFLECT: This afternoon my Maggie came up to me breathlessly excited. "Mommy!" she exploded. "Mommy! I figured out that God is my friend!"

Happy to reinforce such a splendid thought, I replied, "Wow, Maggie! That's great! And you're right—God *is* your friend!" Maggie beamed.

She paused for a moment, then leaned forward confidentially. "Peter's still my *best* friend, Mom. But God's my friend too."

How is it that my almost-three-year-old can turn my thinking upside down so fast? In less than a minute, she's got me wondering: *Is Jesus just one of my friends, or is He my best friend?* To be perfectly honest, I don't always talk to Him as much as I talk to others I trust. Nor is He always the one I turn to first. Would I gladly lay down my life for Him if I had to? I hope so. But then why is it so hard to simply hand over today?

—JULIA ATTAWAY

PRAY: *Dearest Friend Jesus, teach me to be even half the friend to You that You are to me.*

DO: Come to Jesus as your friend, as well as your God and Savior.

WHEN YOU NEED A LIFT

◅◦▻

READ: *I will lift up my eyes to the hills—where does my help come from?*

—PSALM 121:1 (NIV)

REFLECT: Since the very time they were shaped by the hands of the Maker, it has been the ministry of the hills to lift men's hearts to God. Centuries ago they caused the thoughts of a lonely shepherd named David to ignite and flame into worship, and a psalm was born.

But God knew there would be times in our lives when, because of a weight in our hearts or on our shoulders, our eyes would be downcast. He wanted us at those times to be able to see a reminder of His love, and so He consigned to the shadowy valleys some of His most beautiful full-of-wonder creations . . . starlight reflected in a stream seen only by those with bowed heads; earth-hugging flowers so small that they must be viewed from a bent-knee position.

Look up, then, with gratitude—and look down with hope.

—MILDRED BROWN DUNCAN

PRAY: *Even when I'm looking down, Lord, I want my eyes to be on You.*

DO: Be grateful for all the beauty you see looking up or down.

WHEN YOU NEED A REFUGE

◄◊►

READ: *The Lord is my light and my salvation; Whom shall I fear? The Lord is the strength of my life; Of whom shall I be afraid?*

—PSALM 27:1

REFLECT: My tree house was high up in an old apricot tree in the yard of my childhood. The floor consisted of roof shingles, and the single piece of furniture was a gnarled tree branch that curved over the edge of the roof, on which I could sit.

When I had been spanked or scolded, I would climb my tree and sit in my little house, holding tight to the soft-bodied doll who was my best friend. High up and hidden, I found escape.

Today—with inflation, taxes, panic—I still have a refuge. It no longer nestles among leaves and branches. It is neither an escape nor a hiding place. Rather, it is a haven deep within me. Its floor, the everlasting arms of my Father; its walls, the love of dear ones; its roof, the promise of eternal life.

Whom, then, shall I fear?

—DORIS HAASE

PRAY: *I run to Your everlasting arms today, Father.*

DO: Find a quiet haven where you can rest in God's arms.

WHEN YOU NEED A SMILE

◄○►

READ: *The Lord make His face shine upon you, And be gracious to you. . . .*

—NUMBERS 6:25

REFLECT: Not long ago, a woman from Pennsylvania told me about the nerve damage that prevented her from smiling. I sympathized because I knew how very much it means for me to be able to smile. For one thing, I like to be smiled *at*, and I find that all I have to do to get one is to give one.

And have you ever realized the power that lies in so effortless a gesture? I'll bet a smile, perhaps when you least expected it, has changed a day for you. I do know that a smile a stranger gave me in an airport once changed a whole week I had been dreading into one that was richly rewarding.

Even when you don't feel like it, go ahead and smile anyway. By the time you get one or two in return, the magical thing is that you *will* feel like smiling.

—RUTH STAFFORD PEALE

PRAY: *Lord, today I'm going to try to give more smiles than I get.*

DO: Make an effort to smile at as many people you can today and keep track of how many smiles you get back.

WHEN YOU NEED ASSURANCE GOD IS WITH YOU

——◄○►——

READ: *Do not fear, for I am with you.*

— GENESIS 26:24

REFLECT: We once bought a pup—a border collie named Duffy. Because we lived in town, Duffy couldn't run at will but got his exercise in the backyard or on a leash. He particularly looked forward to jogging with me in the morning, but, like many young dogs, was easily spooked by loud noises, roaring chain saws and passing cars.

If he got nervous, I'd draw in on his leash and pull him closer to my pants leg. Then I'd speak to him in a quiet voice: "It's okay, Duffy. Don't be afraid. I'm right here." When I did this, his ears relaxed and he settled back into a smooth stride.

It's good to have a Master to Whom one can draw close when worries and fears abound. It's good to have Someone whisper our names and say, "It's all right, don't be afraid. I'm right here."

— FRED BAUER

PRAY: *Father, knowing You always walk with me, even when I've strayed slightly, calms my worries and fears.*

DO: Find as many Scriptures as you can of Jesus' reassuring words, "I'm right here."

WHEN YOU NEED COMFORT

◄○►

READ: *Search from the book of the Lord, and read....*

—ISAIAH 34:16

REFLECT: "When should we especially read God's word?" The question—posed to our Bible-study group—hung in the air unanswered.

Aunt Mollie, our senior member, pulled a crumpled envelope from her knitting bag and began to read.

WHEN in sorrow (John 14).

WHEN people fail you (Psalm 27).

WHEN you have sinned (Psalm 51).

WHEN you need courage for a task (Joshua 1).

WHEN God seems far away (Psalm 139).

WHEN you need rest (Matthew 11:28–30).

WHEN you feel bitter (I Corinthians 13).

WHEN you are lonely or fearful (Psalm 23).

The Bible is timeless. It lives through generation after generation. It is there any hour of the day or night to comfort and inspire us. We can turn to it as we do to our dear Father—Who is there for us twenty-four hours a day!

—JUNE MASTERS BACHER

PRAY: *Father, I struggle too often when I know Your strength for every situation is in Your Word. I'll look for You there more often.*

DO: Search your Bible with a specific need for yourself or someone else.

WHEN YOU NEED
COURAGE TO GO ON

<o>

READ: *Come boldly to the throne of grace, that we may obtain mercy and find grace to help in time of need.*

—HEBREWS 4:16

REFLECT: Veronica Morgan was one of the first women engineers in our country. She had a brilliant scientific mind and became a senior vice-president of one of the world's largest communications companies.

Sitting next to her at a dinner party once, I asked her what she had been up to. Well, she said, she was keeping busy. She was learning all she could about space satellites. She was representing our government as a consultant to underdeveloped countries. And, oh yes, she had had a mastectomy. But she was fine now and even back to playing her usual poor game of tennis.

Asked where she got the courage to do so many things that had never been done before, Veronica said, "It was given to me—by God. He gives us all we ever need."

—PHYLLIS HOBE

PRAY: *Forgive me, Father, for focusing on my problems rather than Your power in me to overcome them.*

DO: Resume a project or hobby you've given up because of trying circumstances.

WHEN YOU NEED DIRECTION

---◄o►---

READ: *I am with you always. . . .*

—MATTHEW 28:20

REFLECT: I got lost the first time I drove by myself across Albuquerque at night after moving to New Mexico. Panic shivered through me when I realized I'd wandered into a section so dark I could no longer see landmarks or street signs. I couldn't even tell in what direction I was headed.

Frightened and desperate, I whispered, "Lord, I need Your help. Please, show me how to get home."

That's when I remembered: Sandia Crest, the mountain that looms east of the city, has a light on top. I peered through the car windows, trying to find that light among the thousands of stars that twinkled in the midnight sky. Yes, there it was, a steady point of light, unmoving, unchanging, a beacon I could follow.

My shivering stopped, replaced by the assurance of Jesus' guidance, which is available to me wherever I go.

—MADGE HARRAH

PRAY: *Let me always be looking for Your guiding light, Lord.*

DO: Be a light that leads a lost friend to Jesus.

WHEN YOU NEED GOD'S GUIDANCE

◄○►

READ: *I will make darkness light before them, And crooked places straight.*

—ISAIAH 42:16

REFLECT: I took my seat in a small local theater. Pesky worries whirled in my head. *Should I take early retirement from my part-time nursing job? How will I support myself?* So many life-changing decisions.

The theater darkened. The curtains on the stage parted. A beam of light illuminated the stage. *Lord, light up my life like that,* I thought. *I need more light to make wise decisions.*

Halfway through the first scene, an usher came down the aisle, guiding two latecomers. The flashlight he held formed a small circle of light at their feet. Slowly, he moved ahead to the appropriate row; then he shone the light onto two vacant seats.

That's how I lead you! The thought was crystal clear, as though I heard God speaking. *As you read My Word and obey it, you'll have enough light to know what step to take next. And then there'll be more light for the next step, and the next. Trust Me.*

Thankfully, I relaxed and enjoyed the rest of the play.

—HELEN GRACE LESCHEID

PRAY: *Lord Jesus, You are Light and I will seek You more than I seek answers from You.*

DO: Ask the Holy Spirit to guide your Bible reading until you find something that applies perfectly to the decision you're trying to make.

WHEN YOU NEED GOD'S HELP

---◄◦►---

READ: *O Lord my God, I cried out to You,*
and You healed me.

—PSALM 30:2

REFLECT: Once I decided religion was not for me. I was a supremely confident sophomore in college. I'd grown up in the church, but decided I was now too smart for it.

Then, in the dead of winter, with finals looming ahead and six term papers to be completed, my anxiety became enormous. I would stare out of the windows of the library for hours, watching snow flurries, praying to the wind to help me pass.

Praying! To the wind? In my unbelief I had turned consciously to prayer. Why? Because I needed help.

I picked up my books and left the library. I walked across the courtyard to the chapel and, in the silence of that Gothic structure, I prayed to a very real Presence.

With His help, I passed my exams. With His help, I graduated from college two years later. With His help, I go through life. Without Him, I would be lost.

—RICK HAMLIN

PRAY: *Father, draw college students to Yourself who are*
convinced they don't need you.

DO: Offer your help to a college student who has decided he/she is too smart for God.

WHEN YOU NEED GUIDANCE

READ: *Give ear and hear my voice, listen and hear my speech.*

—ISAIAH 28:23

REFLECT: After years of volunteering with the Parents' Association at my children's school, I was asked to be its president, a two-year commitment with much responsibility. When I prayed about it, I didn't feel any urging from God. Just a nudge to ask others what they thought.

My mom was thrilled. "You have to say yes." My husband Paul was pleased. "You love volunteering at school," he said. "You could do a lot of good." And my kids thought it was way cool. "You'll get your picture in the yearbook now."

Even with their support, I still wasn't sure what God wanted me to do. Then one day, sitting on my back-porch swing (my favorite prayer spot), it finally came to me: *I sent all these people who know you and love you to give you advice. What more do you need?*

God often speaks through the people in my life. I needed to listen to them. I got up and made a couple phone calls . . . to accept the job, of course!

—GINA BRIDGEMAN

PRAY: *I can make hearing from You so much more difficult than it needs to be, Father. Thank You for getting Your message across anyway.*

DO: God won't necessarily guide you the same way every time. Ask how He wants you to do it *this* time.

WHEN YOU NEED HOPE

◄○►

READ: *I will hope continually, And will praise You yet more and more.*

—PSALM 71:14

REFLECT: An older man in our small town, an accomplished artist and painter, spends his retirement days hitchhiking in and out of town. Along the way he picks up trash on the highway. Standing along the roadway with his thumb thrust upward, he is a familiar sight. He never waits long for a ride and his many friends look out for him.

One gray day I gave him a ride north. Along the way we passed a high ridge where a strong wind had recently torn off the tops of many trees. Seeing the white scars of the broken limbs, I commented on how sad the scene was.

My friend replied, "Just think about how glorious next spring will be when new growth pops out to replace those scars."

It came to me that my view was focused only on what could be seen while his was on what could be. That started me on a conscious effort to view the world with hopeful eyes.

—ERIC FELLMAN

PRAY: *You give the gift of new life out of death and destruction. Thank You, Father.*

DO: Focus on a situation that seems hopeless and try to look ahead to the good that might come out of it.

WHEN YOU NEED PRAYER SUPPORT

<o>

READ: *Lord, teach us to pray.*

—LUKE 11:1

REFLECT: One Sunday, our Sunday school teacher asked us to pray for his son-in-law, who was facing critical brain surgery the following day. "He has the best brain surgeon in the area," he said, "but without the prayers of those who care, we don't feel that we have the whole team in the game. Will you be a team player with us?"

A year later, in the hospital for a coronary bypass, I remembered his words. I had the best surgeon in the area, but as I looked around the walls of my room, I had proof of something else: Those who cared for me were also praying for me. Our daughter Nancy had covered my walls with colorful handmade posters from the children of the church. And my wife Barbara was holding a stack of prayer cards written and signed by the adults. By their cards and posters, they had demonstrated their commitment to pray. They had all joined the team.

—KENNETH CHAFIN

PRAY: *Lord, I'm so grateful You're on my team. Would You bring a few others to join us who believe in Your power to answer prayer?*

DO: Have someone gather others around to pray with you through a crisis.

WHEN YOU NEED
QUIET TIME WITH GOD

<o>

READ: *I waited patiently for the Lord; And He inclined to me, And heard my cry.*

—PSALM 40:1

REFLECT: We were looking forward to spending time together at a woodsy retreat grounds beside a lake. However, I didn't expect the type of solitude that our leader proposed immediately upon our arrival. He announced, "While we spend these two days together, we will not speak to one another except at mealtime. This is an opportunity to look into God's Word undisturbed by others and to let Him speak to our hearts."

At first I was averse to the idea. Give up fellowship with friends whom I never see enough of anyway?

But then I recalled that Jesus Himself often retreated too—from His disciples, His best friends—to go into the wilderness or a garden to pray.

If Jesus needed time apart, why shouldn't we?

Whether you live alone or with a boisterous, busy family, try giving your spirit a chance to privately and lovingly listen to God as He speaks directly to you . . . and you alone.

—ISABEL WOLSELEY

PRAY: *It amazes me that You long to speak to me, Lord, and even more amazing that I resist making time to be with You when I so long to hear Your voice. I'm listening now, Lord.*

DO: Find an organized retreat or create your own silent retreat to listen for God's voice.

WHEN YOU NEED QUIETNESS

◄◦►

READ: *Surely I have calmed and quieted my soul, Like a weaned child with his mother, Like a weaned child is my soul within me.*

—PSALM 131:2

REFLECT: Twenty-five kindergartners make a lot of noise. When I helped out at our son Scott's school, my voice rose louder over the din. That wasn't the teacher's way! Mrs. Dietz would make her announcements in a whisper.

Near her, a few children, straining to hear, would shush others, shouters would be poked and a wondrous hush would descend on the room. Because she spoke so quietly, the children's listening had an alert, breathless attentiveness.

When, years later, I began praying for guidance, I thought of Mrs. Dietz. God will not raise His voice to be heard above the racket of my life. He wants me to shut off the TV, lay down the newspaper. He calls me to a room alone, then waits for the inner commotion, too, to subside. He will not shout down the conversations in my head. Like Mrs. Dietz, He speaks more softly than them all, until they cease their chatter.

Then, quiet without, quiet within, I listen for the still, small voice that spoke the world into being.

—ELIZABETH SHERRILL

PRAY: *Help me carve a quiet time from this active day, Father, when I can listen for the whispers of Your love.*

DO: Practice lowering your voice when you speak today.

WHEN YOU NEED STILLNESS

◄○►

READ: *Set your heart and your soul to seek the Lord your God.*

—1 CHRONICLES 22:19

REFLECT: One afternoon I went for a long walk along a woodland path. Not even a bird sang, and gradually I became immersed in stillness. As I rested quietly on a huge stone, I actually felt the living presence of God surround me.

I realize that in these days I am seldom still; I have a husband, children and a career. And yet I need to remember: When the children clamor for attention . . . be still, and know that I am God. When I feel that I have not enough hours . . . be still, and know that I am God. When I am overwhelmed by my own inadequacies . . . be still, and know that I am God.

And I have a little exercise that helps: I perch on a footstool, close my eyes and allow God's presence to fill me. Stillness surrounds me, and with my spirit renewed, I'm ready to resume the tasks ahead.

—PATRICIA HOUCK SPRINKLE

PRAY: *Living God, let Your presence surround me.*

DO: Sit in your favorite spot, close your eyes and allow God's presence to fill you.

WHEN YOU NEED
TIME ALONE WITH GOD

◄○►

READ: *When He had sent the multitudes away, He went up on the mountain by Himself to pray. Now when evening came, He was alone there.*

—MATTHEW 14:23

REFLECT: Tonight is mine. The one night when I'll be alone. No work at the desk. No meetings about anything, anywhere. No shopping. No trip to the mall. No movies or television. Just beautiful hours I can use as I please. I can read that book I've neglected. Maybe I'll just sit and think. Perhaps I'll take a walk where there's little traffic or people, where I can really study God's marvelous firmament and feel His peace—that wonderful contentment we seem to have lost.

I believe my love of family and friends is made stronger and more meaningful by standing aside for a time to appreciate those relationships. Being alone, really alone, for a while restores my sluggish mind. To withdraw from my usual routines and to discover new capacities within myself is a cleansing experience. It is a time when I am alone with Christ.

—WALTER HARTER

PRAY: *Lord Jesus, I know many people who need and even desire the cleansing experience of being alone with You. I pray that You would make that desire irresistible.*

DO: Make every effort to get an evening alone with God, sooner rather than later.

WHEN YOU NEED
TO APOLOGIZE

‹◇›

READ: *If we confess our sins, He is faithful and just to forgive us our sins....*

—1 JOHN 1:9

REFLECT: When my son Andrew was eleven, he was on the phone with his older sister Jeanne, an art student in California. I kept talking to him in the background. "Find out what she'd like for her birthday." And, "Ask how her classes are."

Finally Andrew said, "Mom keeps talking, and I can't hear you, so I might as well hang up." He handed me the phone and went off to bed. It took me by surprise. I hadn't meant to ruin his phone conversation.

Half an hour later, I went to his bedroom. As I pulled up the covers, he said. "I'm sorry, Mom. I didn't mean to hurt your feelings."

Andrew was saying "I'm sorry" to a mother who should have said it to him. As I apologized, I realized that those were two words I hardly ever said.

The next time an incident called for it, I would be ready to take responsibility for apologizing. —PATRICIA LORENZ

PRAY: *Lord, give parents courage to apologize when it's what they should do.*

DO: Apologize to someone for not apologizing when you should have.

WHEN YOU NEED
TO BE UPLIFTED

◄◦►

READ: *They shall mount up with wings like eagles....*

—ISAIAH 40:31

REFLECT: A young minister in our town asked some of us to describe the role we'd like to have God play in our lives. "In just one word," he said.

An interesting collection of words came forth: Protector, Redeemer, Guide, Comforter, Friend and so on. But there was one unexpected reply. "I'd like Him," this man said, "to be my Chauffeur."

All of us were taken aback until he explained his choice. "When hot-air ballooning was invented some two hundred years ago in France," he said, "the man in charge of the fire underneath the balloon that produced the hot air was known as the chauffeur, from the French word *chauffer*, meaning, to heat. Without the work of the chauffeur, the balloon couldn't soar. It couldn't even rise.

"I like the thought of God breathing His life-giving Spirit into me every single day so that I can rise above trials and difficulties and preoccupation with material things. Without the lift that God supplies I can do nothing."

—ARTHUR GORDON

PRAY: *Lord, help us to seek and find the power that comes to those filled with Your Holy Spirit.*

DO: Every day ask God to fill you anew with His Holy Spirit.

WHEN YOU NEED
TO CONFESS

◄◦►

READ: *If we confess our sins, He is faithful and just to forgive us our sins and to cleanse us from all unrighteousness.*

—1 JOHN 1:9

REFLECT: "All right, *I'll* put them to bed!" I grumbled. Frightened little faces glanced around the table through the hostile energy that surrounded their parents.

Later, I sat on the edge of my daughter's bed. "All right," I said sternly, "let's say our prayers."

I began, "Dear Lord, bless Mommy, Daddy...."

Silence. Then a miniature echo of my words.

With a start, I realized that my prayers with the kids were never about what was really going on in my life.

Confess, a voice in my head said firmly.

So I began again, "Dear Lord, forgive me for being controlling and trying to boss Mommy around. Help me not to do that."

Silence. Then a tiny voice: "Dear Lord, forgive me for tinkling under the big tree in the backyard last summer."

My daughter prays with her own children now. I hope that she remembers my honest confession the way I remember hers.

—KEITH MILLER

PRAY: *Father, I confess my sin of _____ to You today. Please forgive me and cleanse me from all unrighteousness.*

DO: If the sin you just prayed about involves another person(s), confess to that person(s) as well.

WHEN YOU NEED TO HEAR "I LOVE YOU"

READ: *My little children, let us not love in word or in tongue, but in deed and in truth.*

—1 JOHN 3:18

REFLECT: From the day I walked down the aisle and said, "I do," I expected my husband to say, "I love you" on a regular basis. He lived up to my expectations for a while. And then I began to notice that the "I love yous" were becoming fewer. *He doesn't care much anymore,* I decided. *The honeymoon is over.*

One day as I sat brooding in church, suddenly the minister's words pierced my inattention. "You must learn to listen for love," he said, "because people express it in so many different ways. All of us have to learn how to watch and listen."

And so one evening when my husband casually said, "I passed a kid selling roses on a corner but I was in the wrong lane to stop," I realized, to my surprise, that he had just said, "I love you."

Now I find myself surrounded by love because I've learned to watch—and listen.

—DORIS HAASE

PRAY: *Lord Jesus, Your death on the cross spoke love in the most powerful way possible. Help me to lay down my life—my own choices, preferences and desires—as an expression of my love for others.*

DO: Express your love with words and show it with your actions.

WHEN YOU NEED TO LEAVE A MISTAKE BEHIND

◄○►

READ: *We also rejoice in God through our Lord Jesus Christ, through whom we have now received the reconciliation.*

—ROMANS 5:11

REFLECT: I'm a six-year-old practicing my scales: F, G, A, B— oops, wrong note. I'm about to start over.

"Wait a minute, Teresa." My piano teacher stops me. "You made a mistake," she says. "Good! Just go right on and no one will notice."

During my junior year in college, I lied to a friend. It was a serious lie that eventually destroyed our love for each other. For two years I grew more depressed. Though I asked for forgiveness from God and my friend, I hated myself.

Then one Sunday I sang a solo for church. My heart wasn't in it because I didn't feel worthy. On the second verse I made a mistake, but, true to my training, I kept going.

Then it struck me. Yes, I had made a mistake. But it was time to leave it behind. Every time I started to berate myself, I stopped and told myself, *You are forgiven.*

—TERESA SCHANTZ

PRAY: *I choose to forgive myself, Father, the way You've forgiven me.*

DO: Refuse every thought of the past mistakes you've made right.

When you need to share your burdens

———◀◉▶———

READ: *Two are better than one . . . For if they fall, one will lift up his companion.*

—ECCLESIASTES 4:9–10

REFLECT: It was a tough day. Work was stressful. I was still coping with my divorce, and earlier that day my two-year-old son Harrison had taken a tumble. He was okay, but the whole thing shook me up. I decided to give my minister, who happens to be my father, a call.

"You know, Brock," he said, "I'll bet some of your peers are struggling too. Why don't you form a support group? I'd be glad to join you."

I agreed to try, but I was still nervous when my friends met at my house for dinner. But when I described my dad's idea, the response was immediate. "Things have been so stressful," one friend said. "I can't tell you guys how much I could use this."

We talked for hours. By the time we said good night, it was clear that I wasn't alone with my struggles. Each of us needs help finding God in the confusion of life. Sharing with friends is a good place to start. —BROCK KIDD

PRAY: *Forgive me for being too proud to admit my needs, Lord. And thank You for friends who are happy to share theirs.*

DO: Find a friend or two who could use a prayer/support group.

WHEN YOU NEED WISDOM

◀◉▶

READ: *If any of you lacks wisdom, let him ask of God, who gives to all liberally and without reproach, and it will be given to him.*

—JAMES 1:5

REFLECT: When my wife Joy took a part-time job, the house began to look like a disaster area. One day it got to be too much for overworked Joy. What could we do? I'd tried reasoning with our adolescent sons, and it wasn't working. With a sigh and a "flash prayer" asking for wisdom, I faced the three culprits. "All right, no more living like slobs. From now on, no one will pick up anything for you. Things left out after bedtime will disappear!"

That first night three dollars and two favorite toys disappeared off bedroom floors. More disappeared the next day. But after five days, my sons had the neatest bedrooms in town—and a dad who'd learned a little more about parenting from his Heavenly Father.

Do you need wisdom right now? Stop and pray. The Bible says "He gives generously to all." All we have to do is ask!

—ERIC FELLMAN

PRAY: *I'm so grateful, Father, that You have the wisdom I need (and don't have) for every circumstance I will ever face.*

DO: Think of a situation you're unsure how to handle. Ask God for the wisdom, words, solution you need and listen for an answer.

WHEN YOU QUESTION GOD'S GUIDANCE

READ: *Now I know in part; then I shall know fully....*

—1 CORINTHIANS 13:12 (NIV)

REFLECT: Working on the needlepoint, I was perplexed. There, in the midst of the pale pink and rosy reds, it called for three big stitches of a dark brownish green. *That doesn't make sense,* I thought. *It will spoil the whole effect.* I started to cover the green spot with red instead, but reluctantly went ahead and did as directed.

When it was completed, I had to smile. The lovely lines of that bit of green formed a graceful stem, as if seen beyond and below the ruffled flower. It was far prettier than it would have been without the stem.

In just such a way the texture of our lives is woven. How often I question the directions God seems to give. But if I have the faith to follow His guidance, I can look back and see the wisdom of those "dark green stitches" in life.

—MAY SHERIDAN GOLD

PRAY: *Thank You, Father, for the tapestry You're making of my life.*

DO: Encourage a friend who is struggling with God's guidance by sharing this story.

WHEN YOU THINK
YOU CAN'T COPE

<hr>

READ: *The Lord is my rock and my fortress. . . .*

—PSALM 18:2

REFLECT: On a trip to Israel, our guide pointed out in the Jericho area some tiny, rabbitlike animals scurrying into crevices in the rockbound hillsides. "Those are coneys," he explained. "They are mentioned in the Old Testament."

He went on to tell us that the coneys are defenseless animals whose only protection against predators is the rocks in which they hide. "Very smart, those coneys," he said, shaking his head. "In those rocks, no large animals could dig them out."

Later I started thinking, *we all could learn from the little coneys.*

When the storm clouds gather and we are not sure how to cope, we can stay out and try to weather the buffeting storm all by ourselves . . . or we can seek a rocklike shelter, where we are safe and protected until the skies clear.

—SAM JUSTICE

PRAY: *Father, show me how to take shelter in You. Give me a word from Your Word to see me through this rough time.*

DO: Provide a safe place for a friend who is having trouble coping. Speak an encouraging word; share a Scripture; pray for and with him/her.

WHEN YOU WANT
TO GIVE TO THE POOR

<o>

READ: *Blessed is he who considers the poor; the Lord will deliver him in time of trouble.*

—PSALM 41:1

REFLECT: The clothing rooms operated by our ministry were stocked through lovely handmade donations from generous Christians. But once a woman brought a bag of ripped, threadbare jeans covered with oily stains. Noticing my nose wrinkle (they smelled terrible!) she snapped, "Poor people shouldn't be picky! If they are really in need they'll wear these and be grateful."

That reminded me of a story I once heard. A little girl came home from Sunday school and asked her mother for some food to fill a basket for a poor family. The mother rummaged through the pantry and pulled out a couple cans of anchovies. "Take these," she said. "They've been on the shelf for years, and none of us likes them anyway."

The child's face fell in disappointment. "But, Mother," she said quietly, "if we only share what we don't want, we're not helping the poor. They are helping us."

—PENNEY SCHWAB

PRAY: *Father, I want to give my best to the poor, as if I were giving it to You.*

DO: Take a look at that box of things you have saved up to send to charity. Are you helping the poor by giving, or are they helping you?

WHEN YOU WANT
TO HELP A FRIEND

◄○►

READ: *Mary . . . sat at Jesus' feet and heard His word.*

—LUKE 10:39

REFLECT: I'm a compulsive helper. My good friend Kathy faced a particularly difficult time with a sick daughter, a looming mortgage payment and an out-of-work husband. Of course, I was at the ready with doctor referrals, job applications and offers of a loan. My efforts were stubbornly, if affectionately, ignored.

I was mulling over Kathy's problems during a walk when I noticed a boy and his younger sister riding bikes. Suddenly, the little girl's bike turned over, and she fell with a thud. She looked mournfully at her brother, uncertainty and the beginning of a wail on her face.

Her brother, however, studied the woeful expression for a split second before deliberately spilling his bike in the exact same way. They sat there gazing at each other for a few moments.

Eventually, they got up and began to ride their bikes again.

That evening, I invited Kathy to visit a local park with me. "What for?" she asked warily.

"Just to sit together," I replied.

—MARCI ALBORGHETTI

PRAY: *Lord, help me recognize when it's best just to step back and listen.*

DO: Take a friend to the park, just to sit together.

WHEN YOU WANT TO LET SOMEONE KNOW YOU CARE

---◀◦▶---

READ: *When you do a charitable deed, do not let your left hand know what your right hand is doing, that your charitable deed may be in secret. . . .*

—MATTHEW 6:3

REFLECT: Being a rather shy, unathletic child, I was always uncomfortable during recess when most of the kids played. One cold day in fourth grade, I was standing around feeling self-conscious when one of the most popular girls in my class came over to me. "My hands are freezing," she said, "and my pockets aren't very warm." With that, she plunged both hands into one of my pockets, held them there for a minute, then went back to the game. At noon, when I pulled my lunch money out of my pocket, there was a stick of gum in my hand—a silent message that said, *I care about you.*

A small thing maybe, but I've remembered that quiet little act of kindness all these years. I think what made it so memorable was that she did it secretly, anonymously.

It's a lovely way to say, "I care."

—MARILYN MORGAN KING

PRAY: *God, give a child creativity and the courage to reach out to an outsider today.*

DO: Teach your child(ren) how to say, "I care" with their actions.

WHEN YOU WANT TO SHARE YOUR FAITH

◄○►

READ: *Be kindly affectionate to one another with brotherly love. . . .*

—ROMANS 12:10

REFLECT: "Hey, Brett, I'm speaking tonight at a café for teens. Wanna come?"

To my surprise he said, "I'd love to."

I'd seen him at school, usually standing alone, and had said hi once or twice. For some reason, though, I felt that I should invite him to this event.

We arrived early, so Brett and I played a few games of pool. It felt as if we had been friends forever. That night I talked about what God had done in my life and what it meant to be sure of eternal life.

Over the next two years, we continued our friendship. He even started coming to church. Then one Sunday night, he stood up in front of the youth group. "One day, I became so depressed that I decided to kill myself. But that morning, someone I didn't even know invited me to hear him give his testimony. I changed my mind about suicide and went with him. That night, I gave my life to Jesus."

—JOSHUA SUNDQUIST

PRAY: *Lord, would you give me an opportunity and the courage to share my faith with someone who is desperate to know You?*

DO: Be sensitive and follow through on the first opportunity that comes to share your faith.

WHEN YOU'RE A CAREGIVER

READ: *Who walks in darkness And has no light? Let him trust in the name of the Lord And rely upon his God.*

—ISAIAH 50:10

REFLECT: I was commiserating with my daughter Sandi over the phone. She's a registered nurse, and she'd had a tough day at work. One patient had been especially difficult.

"Is the man having a lot of pain?" I asked.

"No, that's not it. Mr. Jones is just one of those patients who insists on controlling his environment."

"How does he do that?"

"Little things, like continually ringing for a nurse when there's no real need. For instance, he might ring and then ask us to hand him a box of tissues that's well within his reach. Or he worries that we'll forget this medication. Well, tomorrow's another day," she went on, brightening. "Maybe Mr. Jones will relax and trust us to take care of him."

Too many times, instead of trusting God, I insist on telling Him how to handle my problems. Although this must sadden Him, He's always willing to grant me a fresh start.

—BONNIE LUKES

PRAY: *Thank You, Father, for people who are willing to serve others. Give them strength, patience and understanding for those they serve.*

DO: Ask a friend the key to his/her patience for difficult people.

WHEN YOU'RE AFRAID
TO TRY

◄○►

READ: *Show yourself . . . a model of good deeds. . . .*

— TITUS 2:7 (RSV)

REFLECT: I signed up for duty at a children's hospital in Manhattan only to discover I was the world's worst volunteer. My sheltered Alabama childhood had certainly not prepared me to work with city kids from broken homes. After a few months of failing to connect, I was just about ready to give up.

On what was to have been my last night, eight-year-old Victor wanted help drawing a tiger. "Please, somebody," he pleaded, as one by one the volunteers turned him down. "How about you?" He stood in front of me with a brown crayon. I didn't want him to be disappointed, but it was only fair to warn him: "It won't be perfect, Victor."

He frowned and pointed right between my eyes. "Nothing in life is perfect, but you have to try." I looked at that child, whose life had been anything but perfect, and knew he was right. So I tried. And for weeks, a goofy tiger with a lopsided grin hung over my favorite second-grader's hospital bed.

— ALLISON SAMPLE

PRAY: *Lord, I know I'm not perfect, but with my trust in You, I'll try anything.*

DO: That thing you've been convinced you'd fail at—try it.

WHEN YOU'RE ANXIOUS
ABOUT THE FUTURE

◄○►

READ: *We have confidence in the Lord....*

—2 THESSALONIANS 3:4

REFLECT: As a child, whether riding my bike through city streets or scampering along a beach, I wondered what was around the next corner.

This set me on my way to many wonderful adventures, like the time I biked around an unfamiliar corner and came to a field where a baby calf had just been born. But more often than not, it got me into trouble.

One day I urged a childhood friend around "just one more bend of the cove" of our favorite beach. Within minutes we were trapped by the incoming tide. It was a good thing friends came looking for us and rushed for the lifeguards.

As an adult, I am still curious. "I wish I had a futuristic spyglass to see what's around the corner for us," I told my husband over dinner.

"It's a good thing that you don't." He wagged his fork at me, "Leave well enough alone. God has a plan. Trust Him."

—FAY ANGUS

PRAY: *Moment by moment, through every day, I will trust You, Lord, knowing the plans You have for me are good.*

DO: Rather than looking ahead, look back and remember some of the good things God unexpectedly brought into your life.

WHEN YOU'RE ASKING
GOD WHY

◄○►

READ: *It is not good for a soul to be without knowledge. . . .*

—PROVERBS 19:2

REFLECT: My son Andy looked at me with his bright, blue nine-year-old eyes. "Why do we die of old age?"

"Well," I stumbled, "as we age, we grow slower and slower, and then God decides it's time to stop."

"Oh." Then, without a pause, "Why do we taste with our mouth?"

"Because we have taste buds."

"Then do we have smell buds in our nose and hear buds in our ears?"

"I don't think so."

"Why not?"

I handled that one as well as I could and made a quick exit. Andy was in "why mode" and I knew it could go on for hours.

As Andy grew, we enjoyed the increasing complexity of his questions. They revealed a real desire to learn and sometimes challenged us too.

I guess I have my own "whys." And that is as it should be. These endless questions enlarge our understanding and bring us closer to the one true Answer to them all.

—PHILIP ZALESKI

PRAY: *Lord, help me to acquire knowledge and understanding to strengthen my faith and nourish my soul.*

DO: Play the "why game" with your children. Ask them questions about God, the Bible, spiritual issues that will increase their faith.

WHEN YOU'RE AT ODDS
WITH A CO-WORKER

━━━━━━━━━━━━━━━◄o►━━━━━━━━━━━━━━━

READ: *Confess your trespasses to one another, and pray for one another, that you may be healed.*

—JAMES 5:16

REFLECT: The office was small, and I liked everyone I worked with—except Patsy. It wasn't that I disliked her—it was just, well, disinterest.

One morning I happened to take "the Patsy thing" to God. "Lord," I said, "I have the feeling that You are trying to tell me something."

Yes, I am, Eleanor, He answered. *You and Patsy are supposed to be sisters in Christ.* And then I got the distinct guidance that I was to share all this with Patsy.

It was very hard. But one Sunday after church I invited her to my home. We made small talk, then I took a big gulp of coffee and said, "Patsy, there is something I'm supposed to tell you."

I discovered that she had an "Eleanor thing" and didn't know what to do about it! So we spent the afternoon talking and praying, and when she left my apartment we really were sisters in Christ.

—ELEANOR SASS

PRAY: *God, I pray for my brothers and sisters in Christ. Increase our love—and our like—for each other.*

DO: Step out of your comfort zone and reach out to that person who doesn't particularly interest you—yet.

WHEN YOU'RE BLESSED
BY A FRIEND

———————◇———————

READ: *Everyone helped his neighbor, And said to his brother, "Be of good courage!"*

—ISAIAH 41:6

REFLECT: For years my husband and I enjoyed our daily walks together. Sometimes we talked quietly, other times we were just together in silence.

But our walks lost their glow when, after an illness, I *had* to walk as therapy. I suffered with each step. It changed our gait, our buoyancy. Moreover, it was changing my attitude. *What's the use?* I thought. *It's doing no good. . . .*

Then one day a little note arrived in the mail. It said: "Keep it up, you two lovebirds! You make my day as you pass my window every afternoon, looking so fit and happy. I am a shut-in and don't know what I would do without the inspiration you give. 'Things will be better,' your very presence seems to say. . . ."

Each of us is an instrument of God, sometimes inspiring another without knowing it. Today, tell someone you know what they secretly give to you.

—JUNE MASTERS BACHER

PRAY: *Thank You, Father, for friends who are natural encouragers. I'm not one, but I'd like Your help seeing opportunities to say something that would encourage others.*

DO: Be intentional about looking for opportunities to compliment others.

When you're called
on to serve

READ: *I was eyes to the blind. . . .*

—JOB 29:15

REFLECT: For a friend's wedding I reluctantly agreed to look after the groom's blind great-aunt. As I guided the old lady up the walkway to the church, I longed to be with the animated group accompanying the bride to the side entrance.

Once seated, however, the old woman turned out to be a lively companion. As we waited for the service to begin, she peppered me with questions. Was it a Gothic church? Stone! What kind of stone? Was there stained glass? Where was the pulpit located? What color was the seat cushion? Before long I was seeing the church I'd gone to for years with a whole new awareness.

When someone offered to escort the aunt to the reception, I shook my head. I wouldn't have missed her inquiring delight in the guests, the dance steps, the table settings for anything. I wouldn't have missed the insight into God's mysterious ecology either. A very small and grudging kindness on my part had returned to me in blessing.

—ELIZABETH SHERRILL

PRAY: *Open my eyes, Jesus, to the details of life I'm so blind to, like the joy of serving.*

DO: Look at something through someone else's eyes by closing yours and asking questions.

WHEN YOU'RE CHALLENGED TO MOVE OUTSIDE YOUR COMFORT ZONE

READ: *Now when this epistle is read among you, see that it is read also in the church of the Laodiceans. . . .*

—COLOSSIANS 4:16

REFLECT: "I wish you'd write to me sometimes," said my mother, as we lingered over coffee in the restaurant near her retirement home.

"Hey, Mom," I protested, "I phone you every week!"

"Yes," she replied, "but I can't share your calls with anyone. I only remember bits and pieces. . . ."

I felt resentful. Hadn't I just flown halfway across the country to see her? And my weekly calls to her were convenient. Why write?

On my flight back to New York, I pulled out my Bible. When I got to the fourth chapter of Colossians, I read, "After this letter has been read among you, see that it also is read in the church of the Laodiceans."

Only then did I understand Mother's request. I took a piece of stationery and began. "Dear Mom . . ."

—MARILYN MOORE

PRAY: *Even though it takes so much effort, Lord, I can see the value of an old-fashioned letter in a lonely person's life. Help me think more about that than the inconvenience it might be to me.*

DO: Picture the smile and pleasure a letter from you would bring to a loved one. Write it today.

WHEN YOU'RE CLOSING
DOORS FOR YOURSELF

◄◦►

READ: *Jesus said to him, "If you can believe, all things are possible to him who believes."*

—MARK 9:23

REFLECT: When I noticed that the itinerary for the week-long retreat I was attending included chalk drawings, I groaned. I've never been much of an artist.

But as our retreat leader spoke to us about our identity in Christ, she cautioned: "Defining ourselves in terms of what we think we are *not* can be self-defeating, impeding God in us."

So I decided for that one afternoon I would not limit myself. Self-consciously, I dabbed bright yellow pastel onto a piece of newsprint. Soon I began to enjoy the process, adding blue and green and purple to my design. The resulting picture was strangely pleasing, even beautiful. To my surprise, two people later commented that my drawing was their favorite!

My chalk-drawing experience let me see how I close doors for myself by saying, "I can't." From now on I'm going to say, "You know, Lisa, there just might be a new adventure awaiting you. Go for it!"

—LISA ISENHOWER

PRAY: *God, I know I limit You by saying, "I can't."*
If you have a new adventure waiting for me,
Lord, I can do it!

DO: Take one step toward something you think you'd love to do, but are convinced you can't, whether it's buying supplies, taking lessons or reading a how-to book.

WHEN YOU'RE CONCERNED ABOUT YOUR CHILD(REN)'S SAFETY

―◦―

READ: *For he will command his angels concerning you to guard you in all your ways. . . .*

―PSALM 91:11 (NIV)

REFLECT: My daughter Amy Jo elected to take a class that meant she would have a late train ride from Chicago two nights a week. I shivered to think of my petite, blonde girl walking alone on the dark city streets.

On one of Amy Jo's class nights, I seemed to hear a voice commanding: *Pray for a guardian angel!* So I did. "Please, God, send a guardian angel to walk to the train station with Amy Jo tonight."

Next morning, I couldn't wait to talk to Amy Jo. "Any trouble getting to the train station?"

She broke into a wide smile. "Nope! I had a guardian angel!" On impulse, she'd paused at the door of the classroom and asked if anyone might be planning to catch a train.

"Yo, that would be me!" one of the biggest men in the class said. And he walked with Amy Jo all the way to the door of her train.

―MARY LOU CARNEY

PRAY: *Thank You, Father, for divine protection in all its varied forms. Help me to trust my children to Your care whether they're newborn or full grown.*

DO: Pray for guardian angels around all your loved ones.

WHEN YOU'RE CONCERNED FOR YOUR CITY

---◄○►---

READ: *I have many people in this city.*

—ACTS 18:10

REFLECT: While I was visiting Los Angeles, there was a major earthquake. Amazingly, I had experienced two major earthquakes since moving to California several years earlier. Later, when I told a friend that I had been in San Francisco during the Loma Prieta quake too, she said, "Oh yes, I prayed for San Francisco after that, and I prayed for Los Angeles as well."

"You prayed for an entire *city*?"

She smiled and shrugged. "Why not? Cities are made up of people. When I read of some horrific tragedy—a flood, an earthquake—I ask God to heal the city and the people in it."

Although I must admit the idea sounded a little grand to me, I did feel comforted by the idea that she'd been praying for those cities.

Is there a city you would like to ask God to watch over? Perhaps your own?

—LINDA NEUKRUG

PRAY: *Mighty God, show Yourself powerful in cities in crisis today.*

DO: Pray for your city: its residents, its government officials, its economy, that God would be God of it all.

WHEN YOU'RE CONSUMED WITH SELF

◄◦►

READ: *Will they not teach you and tell you, And utter words from their heart?*

—JOB 8:10

REFLECT: As a Chinese scholar lectured, his student kept interrupting with, "Oh, yes, that's familiar to me. I already know the point you're going to make." After a frustrating morning the learned man poured his student a cup of tea. But, even when the cup was full, the sage continued to pour.

"Stop!" exclaimed the know-it-all. "My cup is full!"

"I know," agreed the teacher. "That's your trouble. I can't pour anything into a cup that's already full. Unless you offer me an empty cup, you'll never enjoy my tea."

All too often I find my cup filled with myself—my desire for understanding, appreciation and self-expression. "Me, me, me!" my full cup shouts. Yet it's only when I hold up an empty cup for God to pour His love into in full measure that I begin to have real understanding—of others, and of myself.

—MANUEL ALMADA

PRAY: *Lord, I know I'm often too full of myself to receive from You or others. Please keep pouring until I'm full of You.*

DO: Put a cup and saucer in a prominent place where you can see it often to remind you to be fillable.

WHEN YOU'RE DISAPPOINTED WITH LIFE

◄◦►

READ: *For whatever things were written before were written for our learning, that we through the patience and comfort of the Scriptures might have hope.*

—ROMANS 15:4

REFLECT: My sister Becky had a co-worker who asked for her famous Never-Fail Fudge recipe. Becky gave it gladly, stressing the importance of following the directions to the letter. Later, the woman said she was disappointed with the results.

"Did you boil the chocolate for exactly six minutes?" Becky asked.

"Yes," the woman began, nodding. Then she stopped. "Well, somebody came to the door . . . but I'm sure it was close to six minutes in all."

"Hmm. And you didn't use a beater?"

"No . . . well," her friend confessed, "just for a few seconds!"

Becky was beginning to get the picture. But the woman never did.

How often are we disappointed because we've failed to follow God's never-fail recipe for life? "Trust in the Lord . . . and lean not on your own understanding." "Be content with what you have." Such simple directions that, when not followed, can ruin a moment, a day, a life. —LUCILE ALLEN

PRAY: *Lord, I'm beginning to get the picture. When I'm disappointed with life, help me see which of Your directions I've failed to follow.*

DO: Ask God which of his Biblical directions would make life more tasty right now.

WHEN YOU'RE DISCONTENT WITH WHAT YOU HAVE

READ: *You shall rejoice in every good thing which the Lord your God has given to you and your house. . . .*

—DEUTERONOMY 26:11

REFLECT: I never understood why my grandmother wouldn't buy a new apron. She would smooth a crease from the faded cotton and say in broken English, "This apron still good."

An immigrant from China, she lost her mother at five; at twelve, she was running her father's household and nursing him as he lay dying in a Cantonese village. As a bride of eighteen, she left for America. When my grandfather's store failed, she sewed at night and raised six children by day.

As an old woman, she seemed awed by the richness of her life and expressed it in the loving way she handled food. Her apron was an emblem of what hard work in America had won her: the ability to feed her family without fear of famine, bandits and flood.

I, who had so much, always wanted more. She, who had so little, was joyously awed by her bounty.

—LINDA CHING SLEDGE

PRAY: *I have so much, Lord, and want so much more. Please forgive me and help me choose to be happy with what I have.*

DO: Think of the things you want and ask yourself, "How necessary is it?"

WHEN YOU'RE ENJOYING
EVERYDAY PLEASURES

◄○►

READ: *Every good gift and every perfect gift is from above. . . .*

—JAMES 1:17

REFLECT: The blustery day only added to the high spirits of the children. For the tenth time, it seemed, I said irritably and too loudly, "Please go outside." Then I yelled after them, "But stay close to the house."

Thankful for the peace, I hurried about catching up on chores. Suddenly I realized that things were too quiet. I ran to the door and saw all three boys playing quietly in a large box that had not been there earlier.

"Look, Mom!" Clay shouted. "Jesus sent us a box!"

I was tempted to explain that the wind must have brought it from the grocery store. Then I was ashamed. How seldom I give Jesus credit for the everyday pleasures of life. A child's expression of gratitude caused me to say a prayer as I went back to my work.

—RUTH DINKINS ROWAN

PRAY: *Thank You, Jesus, for all Your special gifts, especially those I haven't thanked You for because I didn't realize they came from You.*

DO: Write a thank-you note to Jesus for His perfect gifts.

WHEN YOU'RE ENVIOUS
OF OTHERS' MONEY

<o>

READ: *"It is easier for a camel to go through the eye of a needle than for a rich man to enter the Kingdom of God."*

—MARK 10:25

REFLECT: When I first came to New York, an acquaintance told me that to really "make it" here you needed to own a building and have it named after you. More recently, someone told me all I needed was a summer home in the Hamptons, a BMW and a six-figure income.

I was feeling a little sorry for myself when one day somebody (could it have been my wife?) had tucked a slip of paper in with my tuna fish sandwich. It said: "The value of a truly great man consists of his increasing the value of all mankind: Adolf von Harnack. Great church historian. And he didn't have a car. And no buildings were named after him."

Will there ever be a Japinga Building? I doubt it. Does it matter? Not at all. I know now that most great people "made it" by contributing something good to this world, not by getting enough money to buy it.

—JEFF JAPINGA

PRAY: *Father, help me to "make it" in this world. Tell me what good thing can I contribute to others.*

DO: Listen for God's answer.

WHEN YOU'RE FACING
A FEAR

READ: *"Do not be afraid . . . I am your shield. . . ."*

—GENESIS 15:1

REFLECT: A friend once told me that when he was a young-ster he was deeply afraid of thunder and lightning. He looked upon this fear as a personal weakness and he was determined to do something about it.

One night a violent storm swept in over the fields where he lived. Smith got out of bed, put on his raincoat and heavy rubber boots, and went outside. While the thunder rolled and the lightning flashed he walked across a meadow and through a dark wood. When he had trudged half a mile he sat on a fence and turned his face to the wind and rain until the storm quieted. Then he went home, climbed back into bed and slept more peacefully than he had ever slept before.

Thunder and lightning never frightened Smith again. He had laid his fear to rest by following this advice—do the thing you fear, and the death of fear is certain.

—NORMAN VINCENT PEALE

PRAY: *God, show me how to lay my fears to rest.*

DO: Look for opportunities to do the thing you fear until you no longer fear it.

WHEN YOU'RE
FEELING BLESSED

<o>

READ: *Let them praise the name of the Lord,*
For He commanded and they were created.

—PSALM 148:5

REFLECT: Once I was the Sunday dinner guest at a home where a small boy named Dennis was asked to say grace. Dennis bowed his head and asked a blessing, which concluded with, "And most of all, God, thank You for the sugar."

At the time I was amused, but then I began to think of all the sugar God has sprinkled into our lives along with our daily bread. We certainly don't need fiddleneck ferns or buttercups to survive. Brassy blue jays and tiny chickadees are also superfluous. My list of God's extras began to grow rapidly: freckles on little boys' faces, the ability to smile, the warmth of a touch. It wasn't long before I'd concluded that God had used an exceedingly generous hand when He planned this universe.

—RUTH HEANEY

PRAY: *Thank You for life's simple pleasures that You didn't really have to create, God.*

DO: Look around you for blessings you've never noticed before.

When you're feeling like a bad parent

◄○►

READ: *A word spoken in due season, how good it is!*
—PROVERBS 15:23

REFLECT: "If I could do it over again I wouldn't yell," I told my daughters-in-law Patricia and Jerie. It was the first time I'd voiced what had long been a genuine regret. I'd asked God's forgiveness, and our grown children didn't seem to resent me. Still, I knew my short temper had caused them misery.

Later, Patricia said, "I asked Pat what he remembered about his childhood. He remembers your reading *Ferdinand the Bull*, and the time his pig had babies and you sat in the barn with him all night." Then Jerie recalled. "Mike remembers you frying two chickens so he could have all he wanted." My daughter Rebecca remembered the yelling, but also playing "dress up" with my best clothes, and bedtime prayers.

Their kind words helped me do something I suspect many other parents need to do: Forgive ourselves for parenting mistakes. Once I did, I began to enjoy memories of happy times instead of being haunted by sad ones.

—PENNEY SCHWAB

PRAY: *Loving Father, thank You for helping my children remember the best of times and forgiving me for the worst!*

DO: Tell your parents some of the positive things you remember about your childhood.

When you're fretful

<o>

READ: *That My joy may remain in you, and that your joy may be full.*

—JOHN 15:11

REFLECT: Sitting in front of a shopping center waiting for a friend, I was feeling fretful because she was late. The passing parade wasn't helping much—whining children tugged impatiently at their mothers' coats.

Then a mother and her child came out of the store. She was the happiest-looking mother I'd ever seen. And her son was wondrously contented.

The young mother was in a wheelchair and held the little boy in her lap. She rolled them out of the store and, once on the sidewalk, she did a fancy little spin. Round and round they went as the little boy laughed out loud. She did too.

When my friend came I was still smiling and uttered a silent prayer. *Father, teach me again that joy never depends on circumstances.*

—MARION BOND WEST

PRAY: *God, restore Your joy to mothers who have lost it.*

DO: Look around you for joy in others.

WHEN YOU'RE GETTING READY FOR A MOVE

◄○►

READ: *For where your treasure is, there your heart will be also.*

—MATTHEW 6:21

REFLECT: I once clipped a newspaper interview with Chicago art dealer Ruth Volid. "I have taken care," she said, "not to clutter up my space with things that have no meaning in my life."

I found that clipping when I was knee-deep in boxes of books, clothes and dishes, packing to move from Chicago to Atlanta. I can't say that it made me immediately toss out everything, but it did give me a new criterion for keeping things. Not merely "Do I need this?" but "Does this have meaning in my life?"

As we've settled into a new house, a new routine and new friendships, I find myself asking, "Does this have meaning in my life?" I see that if I don't clutter my mind with certain books, my time with certain meetings, my daily schedule with certain errands, I have more time to enjoy my family and more time to do the things that really matter.

—PATRICIA HOUCK SPRINKLE

PRAY: *Lord, help me to move on from the unnecessary to the meaningful.*

DO: Make a friend's move easier by helping to thin out his/her possessions.

WHEN YOU'RE GIVING GOD A HAND

ANSWERING YOUR PRAYERS

<o>

READ: *"For the bread of God is He who comes down from heaven and gives life to the world." Then they said to Him, "Lord, give us this bread always." And Jesus said to them, "I am the bread of life. He who comes to Me shall never hunger, and he who believes in Me shall never thirst."*

—JOHN 6:33–35

REFLECT: For years, when I had a need, I entered my study, closed the door, and sank to my knees. When I was done, I would leap to my feet, rush out and try to give God a hand in working toward my prayer aims. After all, I figured, the Lord helps those who help themselves.

Well, often I found that nothing happened. And sometimes the things I was trying to fix only seemed to become more entangled. Finally I stopped butting my head against the wall and decided I would try surrendering myself to God and to God's answers for me.

As I listened and waited, the answers started to come— not dramatic answers, but tiny ones, woven into the fabric of everyday life.

—OSCAR GREENE

PRAY: *I'm very grateful, Lord, for answers to even the tiniest prayers, woven into the fabric of everyday life.*

DO: No prayer is too small. Go ahead and pray for that seemingly insignificant thing.

WHEN YOU'RE GRATEFUL

◄◦►

READ: *Be thankful to Him, and bless His name.*

—PSALM 100:4

REFLECT: After I had surgery to remove a large tumor behind my eye, I telephoned the churches who had prayed for me to thank them and give a praise report. Because of a new medical procedure, I'd had very little bleeding and my surgeons removed most of the tumor with no nerve damage.

"That's wonderful, Roberta," one lady said. "We'll be sure to put it in the bulletin. We have two columns: 'Prayer Requests' and 'Answered Prayers.' Of course, the request column is always a lot longer."

I couldn't get Barbara's comment out of my mind. How often am I like that in my personal prayer life? My "Please Help Me" column is always much longer than my "I'm Grateful" column.

But I started a prayer journal to record my requests and the ways God answers them. I'm amazed at the many answers to prayer that I long took for granted. Being grateful is such a wonderful place to be, I'm making it a lifelong habit.

—ROBERTA MESSNER

PRAY: *I don't just want to say I'm grateful, Father. Help me to truly be full of gratitude.*

DO: Start your own *Please Help Me/I'm Grateful* prayer journal.

WHEN YOU'RE GRIEVING (1)

READ: *Blessed are those who mourn, For they shall be comforted.*

—MATTHEW 5:4

REFLECT: My son Mark was thirteen when he died from a rare form of cancer of the blood. I'd always gone to the cemetery alone, but one day my husband suggested we take all of our children along when we visited Mark's grave.

Five-year-old Heidi wandered away, then returned holding two fistfuls of white clover. I realized she was the only one who had not brought a gift. Kneeling down, she tenderly positioned the small flowers on her brother's grave. Tears streamed down her cheeks. Soon all of us were weeping together.

Mark's death had left us feeling separated from him, separated, in a way, from one another. Now in our grief we were drawn together as we realized that Mark was still with us and that we still had each other in a closer and stronger way.

"The gift of tears," I once read, "is the best gift of God to suffering man."

—JO LINDQUIST

PRAY: *Father, I take great comfort in knowing that You understand the pain of an early death of a child.*

DO: Pray for families who are facing the loss of a child.

WHEN YOU'RE GRIEVING (2)

READ: *I will turn their mourning to joy, Will comfort them, And make them rejoice rather than sorrow.*

—JEREMIAH 31:13

REFLECT: To relax I went sailing with a group out of Rockland, Maine. Joe was the life of the trip. He had a joke for everything, and everyone was always laughing.

I wasn't interested in jokes and quips, so I had my nose in a book or quietly manned the sheets.

One afternoon, as we waited on a beach for lobsters and corn to steam, I noticed that Joe was sitting alone on the hillside. "That's not like Joe," I observed to his brother Jack.

"No one here knows this," Jack told me, "but six months ago, his wife died of cancer."

Joe had been coping with his tragedy by creating laughter, something everyone could share. We all have our own way of handling pain. Withdrawing is necessary sometimes, but healing can also come when we share ourselves with others. In the reaching out, our "mourning can become joy."

—SAMANTHA MCGARRITY

PRAY: *Lord, give those who are grieving the freedom to grieve in their own way.*

DO: Allow yourself that freedom, even if others won't understand.

When you're having
a bad day

◄○►

READ: *I will bless the Lord at all times; His praise shall continually be in my mouth.*

—PSALM 34:1

REFLECT: Phillip was not the brightest boy in my Sunday school class, but his imagination was fired by the stories of King David. Full of enthusiasm, he set out to write his own version of the shepherd king's life story. Sadly, his abilities were not up to the task. For a long time he chewed his pen; then his face cleared.

"A *lot* of things happened to King David," he wrote. "But no matter if they was good or bad he went strate off and made up a plasm about them."

Phillip's spelling left much to be desired, but his words made me wonder: Do I bring all the happenings of my life—good and bad—to God? Only as I learn that He cares about the ups and down of my every day can I begin to turn prayers into psalms. —GLADYS KNOWLTON

PRAY: *I choose to praise You, God, in good times and bad.*

DO: Go "strate off" and write a "plasm" about your day.

WHEN YOU'RE HOLDING
A GRUDGE

◄○►

READ: *Bless those who curse you, and pray for those who spitefully use you.*

—LUKE 6:28

REFLECT: I had taken my wedding dress and veil to a local dry cleaner to be cleaned and preserved. Five months later, I offered to lend a friend my gown. Opening the yard-long white box, we found the dress carefully wrapped in tissue paper—but no veil.

The dry cleaner refused to replace it. "You should have checked the box when you picked it up." I slammed down my phone, shaking with fury. Six years later, when I passed his store, I still heard his caustic voice and my anger burned again.

Pray for those who mistreat you. "Pray for Mr. B? That disgusting man...." Somehow I couldn't start my usual tirade. I whispered, "Lord, have mercy on him. Please forgive me for holding on to anger."

An icy chunk of snow inside me melted. I had tried to forgive. Nothing worked, and the bad feeling . . . persisted. But finally, now, praying for him washed away my bitterness.

—MARY BROWN

PRAY: *Lord, I pray for _____ today.*
I forgive him/her for the offense I've been carrying for too long.

DO: Assign something to symbolize your grudge, say, a dry cleaning ticket. Close your eyes and picture yourself letting go of it and watching it blow away.

WHEN YOU'RE HOLDING ON TO THE PAST

◄○►

READ: *Assuredly, I say to you, whatever you bind on earth will be bound in heaven, and whatever you loose on earth will be loosed in heaven.*

—MATTHEW 18:18

REFLECT: You've probably heard the story about the scientist who devised a unique trap for capturing jungle monkeys. It consisted of a small jar containing a handful of nuts. The jar had a long, narrow neck so that when the monkey put his paw in and grabbed the nuts, he couldn't get his closed fist back out. Silly monkey. All he needed to do was let go of his loot and he'd have been free!

But who am I to laugh at him when my fist is filled too? Silly me. That embarrassing moment I keep reliving in my mind: Isn't it about time I let go of it? All those meetings that crowd my week: Which ones can I exchange for a little more freedom?

Why not take inventory to see if you're clinging to things you'd be better off without.   —MARILYN MORGAN KING

PRAY: *Lord, I need to let go of _____.
I'll do it today; help me not to stick my hand back in the jar of nuts.*

DO: Take inventory to see what you're clinging to.

WHEN YOU'RE IN CONFLICT WITH YOUR SPOUSE

◄○►

READ: *If it is possible, as much as depends on you, live peaceably with all men.*

—ROMANS 12:18

REFLECT: The phrase "the Man upstairs" took on a whole new meaning for me one morning in our split-level house. My husband Bill and I were like two locomotives racing toward a crossing. Collision was inevitable and I was wondering how to short-circuit the process. I walked downstairs to the lower level, put the laundry in the washer and turned on my laptop.

While the computer booted, I glanced up at the verse-a-day calendar leaning against a broken printer. It was Romans 12:18. I began trying to figure out how it applied to me. Then the phrase, "the Man upstairs" popped into my head.

Yes, I thought happily, *I have peace with "the Man upstairs." Thanks to Jesus, I can live as His child and run to Him in confidence whenever I need to.*

No, the thought came again, *I'm not at peace with, literally, "the man upstairs."* Indeed, I needed to start my peacemaking right here at home, with my "man upstairs." And I went up to tell him so.

—ROBERTA ROGERS

PRAY: *Lord, help households in conflict live in peace with each other.*

DO: Be the first to apologize, even if you're right.

WHEN YOU'RE IN PAIN
AND AFRAID

<o>

READ: *Be still, and know that I am God. . . .*

—PSALM 46:10

REFLECT: Lying on the cold, black slab of the X-ray table, I was terrified. I had taken a fall. It was a bad break. The grim face of the X-ray technician confirmed it.

As the ominous-looking X-ray machine descended over my knee, my fright increased. My pulse resounded in my ears as my heart raced—ka-boom, ka-boom, ka-boom. I gripped the edges of the metal table, fighting back pain and panic. And suddenly, incredibly, a message seemed to come to me, timed to the heavy rhythm of my heart: "Be still—and know—that I—am God."

In moments, thanks to those majestic words of reassurance, I had gotten hold of myself again.

That episode happened years ago. Now, whenever I feel overwhelmed, this little "heartbeat reminder" never fails to reassure me that God is with me and within me, always.

—PATTI PHILLIPS

PRAY: *God, I'm so grateful that Your love surrounds me and Your Word fills me, even in an MRI machine.*

DO: Pass this on to a friend who is hurting and afraid.

WHEN YOU'RE INSPIRED BY SOMEONE'S WORK

READ: ... *not lagging in diligence, fervent in spirit, serving the Lord....*

—ROMANS 12:11

REFLECT: My house was right in back of a stately brick church with magnificent stained-glass windows, each nearly twenty feet high. One summer the windows were being restored and I made a habit of stopping to watch the fellow working on them.

He was nimble on the scaffolding, he whistled or hummed as he worked, and his hands, while quick, seemed almost reverently to caress the glass. Soon he was greeting me with a friendly. "Hey, how are you?" but he'd never pause to chat. His work in the soft, waning afternoon sun was too precious to fritter away in small talk.

What an inspiration he was! At a time when many complain that craftsmanship is as dead as the work ethic, here were both flourishing in my backyard! Perhaps your enthusiasm and energy for the tasks at hand today can be an inspiration to another.

—JAMES MCDERMOTT

PRAY: *I pray, Father, not just that I would witness the work ethic flourishing, but that it would flourish in me.*

DO: Make sure the next job you do is done with enthusiasm and energy, whether it's cooking dinner, cleaning house or creating a work of art.

WHEN YOU'RE IRRITATED
WITH YOUR SPOUSE

◄○►

READ: *Love . . . does not behave rudely, does not seek its own, is not provoked, thinks no evil. . . .*

— 1 CORINTHIANS 13:4–5

REFLECT: My dad has spent his whole life in baseball. No matter what situation comes up, he translates it into a baseball analogy. One of his favorites compares a good umpire with a good spouse.

"A good umpire," he says, "has one eye and one ear. If he saw every gesture or heard everything the players hollered at him he'd be throwing everybody out of the game. A good umpire doesn't notice a lot of little things that he knows would make him mad."

I thought of my dad's advice today when I snapped at my husband over a little inconvenience. Like a good umpire, Paul quietly ignored my behavior until my anger passed. I wonder how many little things he overlooks in loving me— as I hope I do with him.

In looking with just one eye, and listening with just one ear, you catch only the good things. —GINA BRIDGEMAN

PRAY: *No one has ever overlooked offenses like You, Jesus. Thank You for showing us that by Your Spirit, it is possible.*

DO: Thank your spouse when he/she has overlooked your angry behavior.

WHEN YOU'RE LEARNING TO TRUST GOD

READ: *We have such trust through Christ toward God.*

—2 CORINTHIANS 3:4

REFLECT: Our two-year-old granddaughter Jamie was visiting. She scurried ahead of me one evening as we made our way down the stairs to the kitchen for a cookie. She was halfway down the steps before she realized how dark it was.

Just as I rounded the corner behind her, I saw her sturdy little shape. She stood perfectly still, looking ahead, one hand on the banister and the other hand outstretched over her head, waiting for mine.

I paused for a moment and looked at her. She waited so patiently, so calmly. She didn't turn around to see if I was coming, or even call out. She simply stood there, still and quiet, one small hand lifted up.

In the kitchen, I thought: *I must learn to trust my Father in that way. His hand is surely over me.*

All I have to do is reach up with certain faith.

—MARION BOND WEST

PRAY: *I want to stand and wait for You to take my hand, Father, never doubting that You will.*

DO: Observe the level of trust in the children in your life.

When you're lonely

READ: *You will keep him in perfect peace, Whose mind is stayed on You. . . .*

—ISAIAH 26:3

REFLECT: One kind of loneliness intensifies as the years mount. It is the loneliness we feel for those who have gone, whose presence brought so many happy hours of love.

One day, I found myself reading *Alice Through the Looking Glass* to my grandchildren. Alice was very lonely "Oh, don't go on like that!" cried the Red Queen. "Consider what a great girl you are . . . consider what o'clock it is. Consider anything. Only don't cry!"

"Can you keep from crying by considering things?" Alice asked.

"That's the way it's done," said the Queen . . . "Nobody can do two things at once."

The children regarded all this as nonsense, but to me it repeated Isaiah's song. Like the Queen said, I couldn't do two things at once! Keeping my mind on Him brought the peace I sought.

—ELAINE ST. JOHNS

PRAY: *Father, sometimes it's hard to remember that peace can be a choice. Help me choose it today by keeping my thoughts on You.*

DO: Read *Alice Through the Looking Glass* to a lonely child.

WHEN YOU'RE LONGING TO EXPERIENCE MORE OF JESUS

◄◦►

READ: *These are written that you may believe that Jesus is the Christ, the Son of God, and that believing you may have life in His name.*

— JOHN 20:31

REFLECT: When I visited the Holy Land, I went with the hope of having some kind of deep religious experience. There was nothing I did not do to make it happen. I marched clear around Jericho, waded in the Jordan, crept into Lazarus' tomb . . . . Still, the "great experience" eluded me.

Finally, when I had delayed our tour group with a hands-and-knees examination of where the cross of Calvary is thought to have been, our leader took me aside. "I think you're taking all this a bit too seriously," he said.

"I think it's the most serious thing in the world," I returned.

"Yes," he said, "but the serious part is not where Jesus Christ was. The serious part is what He said and did."

That night I picked up my Bible. And there, suddenly, was my "great experience." Christ was there, speaking to me from the pages of Holy Scripture.

— BARBARA H. DUDLEY

PRAY: *I think it would be wonderful, Jesus, to walk where You walked on this earth. But even more, I want to experience You in the pages of Your living Word.*

DO: Seek God with all your heart, right in your own home, in the pages of your Bible.

WHEN YOU'RE LOSING FOCUS

◄◦►

READ: *Let us lay aside every weight, and the sin which so easily ensnares us, and let us run with endurance the race that is set before us. . . .*

—HEBREWS 12:1

REFLECT: "Spit out that gum!" my coach yelled as I rounded the third turn of the 400-meter dash at the high school sectional track meet. She met me at the finish line to make sure her words had gotten through.

"Not bad—sixty-three seconds—but what are you doing with gum?" she cried. "Every effort you're putting into anything besides moving toward the finish line is taking away energy for the race."

For the state meet the next weekend I begrudgingly heeded her advice, partly because I'd do anything to shave even a tenth of a second from my time. I checked the clock after I'd crossed the finish line: sixty seconds! I'd cut off three seconds, just by eliminating one little thing.

I wondered if I was losing focus elsewhere. Since then, I've been on the lookout for all the other things that might be slowing me down and keeping me from my goals.

—ASHLEY JOHNSON

PRAY: *God, help me get rid of anything in my life that is taking my focus off You and what You've called me to do.*

DO: Identify the people or activities that may be causing you to lose your focus for the Lord.

WHEN YOU'RE MAKING
A JOB DECISION

◄○►

READ: *He poured water into a basin and began to wash the disciples' feet. . . .*

—JOHN 13:5

REFLECT: I was a first-class machine operator. I was proud, too, of the plant where I worked, until unexpectedly orders slowed and many machinists were laid off. I was one of them, but I was given special "consideration." I was told I could stay on—if I was willing to sweep floors.

Sweep floors! Me, a college graduate? Me, a proud, skilled man *pushing a broom?* My friends all advised me to quit. My wife, much wiser, advised me to pray. So I did. "What shall I do, Lord?" I asked. And the answer, the quiet answer I seemed to get was: "I washed My disciples' feet, didn't I?"

So I laid pride aside, and I took that broom, and I pushed it. For eight long weeks I pushed it, hating every minute of it. Then, just as unexpectedly, orders picked up again. And I was the first machinist rehired.

—OSCAR GREENE

PRAY: *Thank You, Jesus, for being my example and for speaking when I so need Your guidance.*

DO: Rather than taking friends' advice, even if it's good advice, pray and ask God what He thinks.

WHEN YOU'RE MAKING
AN IMPORTANT DECISION

◄◉►

READ: *Who knows whether you have come to the kingdom for such a time as this?*

—ESTHER 4:14

REFLECT: Long before the TV show *CSI* introduced all of America to the language of crime scene investigations, it was a language I knew. The police-detective father of a childhood friend often talked about his work. His message was the same as the hit TV show: "You never know where you might find the one essential fact that solves the case. So pay attention."

Once I had to decide whether to leave my current job for a new opportunity. The choice was neither easy nor clearcut. There were good reasons to stay and good reasons to go. Frankly, I was stymied.

In the end, I didn't take the new job. But not because my long list of pros and cons finally swayed me in a particular direction. Rather, it was because of a small clue I found in a book I was reading that was about a group of Belgians who helped Jews during World War II—one brief phrase that resounded within me for days: "We chose to stay with those who needed us most."

—JEFF JAPINGA

PRAY: *Your guidance is still real today, God. Open my eyes and heart to those unexpected places of Your leading.*

DO: Look for clues to your answer in unexpected places—a bumper sticker, a voice on the radio, a sign in a shop.

When you're not sure how to pray

READ: *"Father, I thank You that You have heard Me, and I know that You always hear Me. . . ."*

—JOHN 11:41–42

REFLECT: Our daughter's earliest prayers were simple thank-you prayers, and she fell into the habit of beginning every prayer with the words, "Thank You, Jesus." By the time she was five, her prayers were more complex, including petitions for herself and others. But she still insisted on the same formula, with the results that her prayers sounded rather awkward: "Thank You, Jesus, for letting me play with Katy tomorrow." "Thank You, Jesus, that You will give Grandpa and Grandma a safe trip." "Thank You, Jesus, that You Help Mommy's cold get better."

I wondered if I should teach her that not *every* prayer had to begin that way. Yet, as I listened to these prayers, I realized that she was teaching me. She had complete confidence in Jesus. Trusting in Him, she was, as it says in Ephesians, "always giving thanks to God the Father for everything"— even before it happened!

—CAROL ZIMMERMAN

PRAY: *Thank You, Father that* _____.

DO: Fill in the blank above with what you're grateful God is going to do or has done.

WHEN YOU'RE
OVEROBLIGATED

<o>

READ: *But we do all things, beloved, for your edification.*

—2 CORINTHIANS 12:19

REFLECT: Should I? Shouldn't I? Should I? Shouldn't I? Like picking petals from a daisy, I'd debated for weeks about whether to continue on the leadership team of the women's ministry at my little country church.

I had been feeling burdened with obligations—home-educating my daughter, freelance editorial work, and daily family and household demands. *The women's ministry should probably go,* I thought.

Then I received a Christian magazine in the mail. One article was about the apostle Paul and his friendships, which, at first glance, had nothing to do with leading a women's ministry. But one sentence in the article had everything to do with it: Paul "was gripped by a powerful vision of friendship as a catalyst for spiritual growth."

I'm no Paul, but the women at Garden Valley Bible Church *were* dear friends. Suddenly my decision wasn't about an obligation; it was about loving and helping friends grow. Now *that* I have time for.　　　　—LUCILE ALLEN

PRAY: *My time is Yours, Lord. Show me how You want me to use it.*

DO: List your obligations in order of priority and ask God which, if any, should go.

When you're praying
for a loved one

---◄○►---

READ: *Pray without ceasing. . . .*

—1 THESSALONIANS 5:17

REFLECT: I looked up at the clock on my classroom wall one more time. It was one o'clock, and still no word from my son Christopher, who was taking his firefighter certification test —a competitive test that required mental and physical stamina. Christopher had to pass in order to continue his training.

I prayed silently, as I had all morning.

When the final bell rang to signal the end of the school day, I decided to call.

"Oh, hi, Mom," Christopher said. "Sorry I forgot to call you. I got busy here at the fire station after I found out that I'd passed my test."

I was overjoyed, but also annoyed. I had spent the day in constant prayer while waiting for a phone call. Right before I embarked on a "Do you have any idea what my day was like?" lecture, I remembered the advice of a wise friend. "If a problem brings you to prayer, then it has served its purpose."

—MELODY BONNETTE

PRAY: *Gracious and loving God, thank You for turning my problems into opportunities to become one with You in prayer.*

DO: Keep praying until you know your prayer has been answered.

When you're ready
to quit

READ: *"These many years I have been serving you. . . ."*

—LUKE 15:29

REFLECT: "Better *is* than *was*!" read the safe-driving poster. And suddenly I was reminded of a dilemma I had recently been trying to resolve. I had been feeling, perhaps somewhat justifiably, that I had "served my term" in church group activities and taught enough Sunday school classes over the years. But then an inner voice would argue that if I withdrew, wouldn't I run the risk of becoming a "was"? And those around me—at home, at church and at work—still needed me to be an "is." And, oh, I had to admit, how good it was to be needed! All at once my dilemma was resolved by the message on that simple poster. No matter how long your route may seem or how tempted you may be to turn off, keep on going straight ahead and be an "is" for the Lord.

—JUNE MASTERS BACHER

PRAY: *Father, I'm okay with being a "was" in some areas, as long as You give me a place to be an "is."*

DO: Maybe it's time to move on to a new avenue of service before you burn out. Consider some new options.

WHEN YOU'RE READY
TO TEST YOUR LIMITS

———————◄◊►———————

READ: *I can do all things through Christ who strengthens me.*

—PHILIPPIANS 4:13

REFLECT: I was working out at the gym with a weight that usually had me trembling when I got to the fifteenth repetition. This time, I told myself I was going for twenty.

And the strangest thing happened: As soon as I told myself that fifteen reps wasn't my boundary, passing it wasn't a problem. All of a sudden, sixteen wasn't nearly as difficult as fifteen had always been. *Well, how do you like that?* I thought. *Fifteen wasn't my limit after all.*

And wouldn't you know it, while I was having this little inner celebration I heard myself say, "Twenty-one!"

I think it's true that when I give myself limits, my body tends to agree. And I think the same principle applies on the job, in my relationships and in my prayer life. I'll never know how far I can go unless I stop telling myself what I can't do and start swinging for the fences. You never know, I might hit a home run.

—DAVE FRANCO

PRAY: *Lord, I give You permission to stretch me beyond what I think I'm capable of doing.*

DO: Stretch your physical or spiritual boundary today.

When you're searching for God

---◆◇◆---

READ: *Then their eyes were opened and they knew Him. . . .*

—LUKE 24:31

REFLECT: One little fish swimming in the sea had heard about a wonderful thing called "water." More than anything the fish wanted to go off, wherever he needed to go, to learn more about this water.

He was gone for many years. And one day he returned to ·the other fish. Before telling them about his discovery, he said, "You aren't going to believe this!"

The fish had finally realized he didn't need to go anywhere for his discovery. He had been totally immersed in it his whole life.

I recognize myself in that little fish. Sometimes my spiritual striving makes me think that reading more books will bring me closer to God. Or taking more classes. Or going to more retreats. It's as if I think God's presence lies just around the next corner. Perhaps like the little fish, I need to learn that meeting God is not so much a discovery . . . as it is a recognition.

—TERRY HELWIG

PRAY: *Lord, show me how to enjoy Your presence even as I search for more of You.*

DO: Come up with a physical reminder of the nearness of God. A new pet fish, perhaps?

When you're seeking spiritual growth

◄○►

READ: *The kingdom of heaven is like a man traveling to a far country, who called his own servants and delivered his goods to them.*

—MATTHEW 25:14

REFLECT: I could feel it happening to me. Despite the schedule I had set for myself for further spiritual growth—Bible reading, meditation, prayer—I was having trouble staying with my plans. Concerned, I wrote of my problem to the man who had been pastor of our church for many years before his retirement.

"Instead of dedicating parts of your day to God," he wrote, "dedicate the whole day to Him. Meditate while you travel to work. On the job, offer up your efforts for His glory. Keep God's love in your heart in your relations with others, asking forgiveness when you offend, granting forgiveness when you are offended. Let God be your partner in all you do at all times."

Adjusting to this constant companionship with the Lord required considerable effort and frequent reminders, but with Him at my side every step of the way, I began traveling on the right road again.

—GLENN KITTLER

PRAY: *Father, be my partner every minute of every day.*

DO: Rather than giving God slices of your life, walk with Him as your constant companion.

WHEN YOU'RE SINGLE AND LOOKING

◄○►

READ: *Let your conduct be without covetousness; be content with such things as you have.*

—HEBREWS 13:5

REFLECT: Back in the days when I was dating, I was afflicted with envy of happy couples. On one first date, I knew in the first ten minutes at the restaurant that this was not the man for me. And at another table, I saw what appeared to be a blissfully happy couple. The woman was radiant, smiling, holding the man's hand. I felt consumed with envy.

After the man had paid the check, he returned to the table and stood by the woman's chair. One of the waiters brought a wheelchair to the table. The woman reached up, and the man put his arms around her waist and lifted her into the chair.

I stared, ice cold; I had just been blessed with an unforgettable lesson at a time when I most needed it. I couldn't trade my life for only a part of someone else's—I'd have to take it all. I should treasure what I have instead of wasting time coveting what I didn't have. —RHODA BLECKER

PRAY: *Dear God, for all single-and-looking people, help them look with contentment.*

DO: List the things in your life others could envy and give thanks for each one.

WHEN YOU'RE SO WORRIED
YOU CAN'T SLEEP

◄◦►

READ: *He delivers and rescues. . . .*

—DANIEL 6:27

REFLECT: Irritable and sleepless, I thrashed under the covers rehashing the same old problem. I pulled my pillow over my head to shut out the faint strains of someone practicing the piano in the apartment next door. *Tinkle, tinkle, tinkle.* Suddenly I remembered my first piano recital.

The teacher had turned the recital into a party. But that was not going to help me play—without sheet music—Beethoven's "For Elise." When the dreaded moment came I plunged in, but went blank at the halfway point. Desperately, I began again. And again. At last, a hand under my elbow lifted me from the piano bench. "Thank you, Nancy," my teacher said, gently.

I sat up on the edge of my bed. Wasn't I doing the same thing now—obsessively repeating what I already knew because I didn't know what to do next? Why not ask my Teacher to rescue me?

—NANCY S. SCHRAFFENBERGER

PRAY: *Rescue me, please God, from rehashing the same old problem. Let me rest until Your answer comes.*

DO: Come up with a Scripture, song or phrase to rehearse instead of the problem that keeps coming to mind.

WHEN YOU'RE
STILL WAITING

<o>

READ: *Though it tarries, wait for it; Because it will surely come....*

—HABAKKUK 2:3

REFLECT: In junior high, I was a reporter for the school newspaper. I sat behind the bench during basketball games, close enough to see the hope and the anguish that warred on the faces of the benchwarmers.

They wore the team uniform and jacket. They practiced shooting free throws. They ran laps. But still they sat on the bench, waiting. They sold candy and washed cars to raise funds for the team, but week after week, it was never their turn. "Just wait, I'm going to need you," the coach would tell them.

There's a change in my life that I've been preparing for and praying for, and all indications are that it's coming; I just don't know when. I'm anxious and sometimes I feel like going to the locker room and putting on my street clothes. That would be easier than waiting.

Instead I look up toward the heavens. "I trust You, God," I whisper. "Coach, let me in the game!"

—SHARON FOSTER

PRAY: *Lord, help me to be patient until my preparation, my passion and my destiny intersect with Your divine plan.*

DO: Encourage a friend that his/her waiting time is not wasted, but training.

WHEN YOU'RE STUCK
IN THE PAST

‹○›

READ: *Forgetting those things which are behind and reaching forward to those things which are ahead, I press toward the goal.*

—PHILIPPIANS 3:13–14

REFLECT: I was face down on a surfboard off the beach at Waikiki. I had always wanted to try to ride the Hawaiian surf, but among these giant green swells I didn't feel very adventurous.

"Now, face the beach," said the brown-skinned beach boy who had accompanied me on his own board. "When wave lifts board, you paddle hard. Then you stand up."

Stand up? "Tell me," I croaked, "what's the main thing to remember?"

"Don't look back!" he said smiling.

Ahead of me a great chasm seemed to open in the sea. The board tilted down. It plunged deep into an emerald precipice and I tried to stand up. A million seething tons of saltwater were poised above my head. In that instant, I looked back. . . .

Well, I didn't drown. I floated while my board went plunging away.

But I've always remembered what the beach boy said: *Don't look back.* At past mistakes. At lost opportunities. At hurt feelings. No, concentrate on what lies ahead.

—ARTHUR GORDON

PRAY: *Lord, help me to reach out to the challenging future, not look back to the unchangeable past.*

DO: Tape a picture of a surfer riding a huge wave to your bathroom mirror.

WHEN YOU'RE SURPRISED BY LIFE

◄○►

READ: *Wisdom and knowledge will be the stability of your times, And the strength of salvation. . . .*

—ISAIAH 33:6

REFLECT: Surprises—everybody loves them. Or do we? The delightful surprises are the ones I grab for: a baby on the way; a tax refund. Then there are the dubious surprises: My husband breaks his ankle; a black bear rummages through the garbage can. And there are sorrowful surprises: the hospital phoning to say my father had died; a business venture failing.

It's easy to sing when the surprises are fun. But what if they come laced with pain and suffering?

I've found my reason to hope in this Bible promise: "In the world you will have tribulation; but be of good cheer, I have overcome the world" (John 16:33). Here is the stability I need to keep my balance in a teetering world. The peace of His Presence, the joy of His strength, the glory of His name are mine to enjoy. Because He has overcome, so can I . . . and that should come as no surprise!

—CAROL KNAPP

PRAY: *Father, my stability comes from knowing that You aren't surprised by the surprises that come my way.*

DO: Find your own Bible promises that give you balance in a teetering world.

WHEN YOU'RE TEMPTED
TO COMPLAIN

――――――◀◎▶――――――

READ: *Be strong and of good courage.*

—JOSHUA 1:18

REFLECT: One marker in my Bible is a cartoon I found years ago in a magazine I'd taken to lunch with me, planning to read as I waited for a friend.

It had been a downbeat morning. I awoke depressed. My husband Carl had already left for work, so I poured coffee, flipped on the newscast and opened the morning paper. Both depressed me further. A sudden rainstorm made driving to town hazardous. Truckers splashed muddy water onto my windshield, and a driver pulled out from behind me. He then sped around and slammed on his brakes. I was ready to give my friend an earful of the morning's near disasters. Then I opened the magazine.

The cartoon before me depicted a motherly looking woman gazing down affectionately at her dog, a springer spaniel. "Thank you," she was saying, "for not talking about recession, inflation, the weather or your health." I got the message and chuckled. We had a pleasant lunch.

—ALETHA JANE LINDSTROM

PRAY: *I confess my tendency to complain, Lord. Thank You*
for reminders to keep my mouth shut.

DO: Stop yourself and then apologize when you've started complaining to a friend.

WHEN YOU'RE TOO
DISTRACTED TO HEAR GOD

◀◦▶

READ: *Then you will call upon Me and go and pray to Me,*
and I will listen to you.

—JEREMIAH 29:12

REFLECT: Four-year-old Peter was kneeling beside his bed,
saying his goodnight prayers. That is, he was trying to. But
his little sister, age one, was making an insistent effort to
draw attention to herself.

Distracted, Peter began again, "Lord, bless Mommy and
Daddy and . . .

"God can't hear me!" he finally complained to his mother.

"Of course He can," his mother assured him, trying to
shush the baby. "God hears everything."

"Maybe . . ." Peter dubiously agreed. "But I can't hear Him!"

Ah, Peter! One way or another, the din that surrounds
you now will continue all your life. You'll have to learn, as we
all do, to listen for the still, small voice in spite of the din.

—NITA SCHUH

PRAY: *Lord, help me to learn to hear the many ways You*
speak.

DO: Practice quieting your mind and heart and listening to
God in the noisiest circumstances.

WHEN YOU'RE TOO PREOCCUPIED TO LISTEN

◄◦►

READ: *And all Your children shall be taught by the Lord,
And great shall be the peace of Your children.*

—ISAIAH 54:13

REFLECT: Esther, our vivacious teenage daughter, burst into the kitchen after school and waved something at me, "I got a rose!"

"That's nice," I said absentmindedly.

As a refugee sponsor for our church, my mind was mulling over the problems that needed to be solved before our refugee family arrived: Find appropriate housing; stock the shelves with groceries; arrange for daily transportation.

"'Bye, Mom," Esther yelled as she slammed through the back door. "I'll be back at eleven." I watched her little green car shoot off to her after-school job.

Suddenly, my mind snapped to attention. What was it she'd been so excited about? A rose? I hurried into her bedroom and picked up a small vase that cradled a perfect red rosebud. My daughter had received her very first rose from an admirer. She'd wanted to share her precious moment with me, and I let worries get in the way.

When my daughter came home from work, I was determined to do better. "Esther," I said, "tell me about the rose."

—HELEN GRACE LESCHEID

PRAY: *Father, thank You for reminding me that life is too short to zoom past intimate moments with my children. Let me gather them, savor them and store them up for years ahead.*

DO: Give your children permission to ask for your full attention.

WHEN YOU'RE TOO
WORRIED TO SLEEP

◄○►

READ: *I will pray the Father, and He will give you another Helper, that He may abide with you forever. . . .*

—JOHN 14:16

REFLECT: I glanced at the clock on the bedside table. 3:25 AM. I moved silently into the living room. I was tired but my mind wouldn't let me rest and I lay down on the couch, mulling over the affairs of the day.

My son Jeff was in a struggle to pull his life back together following a recent divorce. My parents seemed always to have too much work to do, and not enough time to do it. Neither had been well. And my poor mother-in-law had been in the grip of a serious depression that had affected her entire family. Tonight I wondered what the future held for these people I loved.

I spotted the soft throw that is always folded on the couch. *Pull the comforter over you*, I said to myself. Then I was struck by the phrase I'd just used. Why, of course! What other possible answer could there be for any of life's problems? Resting . . . safe in the arms of the Comforter.

—LIBBIE ADAMS

PRAY: *Lord, would You comfort people who are too worried to sleep tonight.*

DO: Rest in the arms of the Comforter.

WHEN YOU'RE UNHAPPY

◄○►

READ: *We count them blessed who endure.*

—JAMES 5:11

REFLECT: She was eighty-seven; he was a year older. They'd had their full share of the good in life as well as the troubles: the turbulent passages of marriage, the children who disappointed them, the illnesses. One afternoon she came upon him in their living room, sitting in "his" chair by the fireplace, but there was no book on his lap, as was usual at that hour. He was simply sitting.

"Anything wrong?" she asked, gently.

"No. I was just thinking."

"Thinking?"

"Yes. About how happy I am."

My dear old friend Jane mentioned this tiny incident to me long ago. It makes me wonder if we don't have too great an expectation of happiness.

Maybe we should stop . . . now, this minute . . . and look to see if happiness is here.

—VAN VARNER

PRAY: *Father, help me find happiness in the simple things around me.*

DO: Stop now, this minute, and look around for small things that make you happy.

WHEN YOU'RE UNSURE OF GOD'S VOICE

---◄◦►---

READ: *Out of heaven He let you hear His voice, that He might instruct you. . . .*

—DEUTERONOMY 4:36

REFLECT: My wife Tib can identify a great many birds by their songs. She's worked hard to gain this skill, listening to recorded birdcalls, studying graphs of characteristic song patterns. In the field she is uncanny.

On a recent spring walk, she'd stop, listen, point. "A veery! Do you hear it?" "Listen, a yellow throat." "That was a song sparrow." Where I heard only a cacophony of warbles and trills, she distinguished wrens, catbirds, towhees, finches —a total of seventeen species.

Over the years, with her help, I have learned to identify a few birds by their calls. It's a valuable ability in the world of the Spirit too. I hear a chorus of voices calling to me from every direction. Which is God's, which are other people's, which is my own? The more I practice listening in prayer, the more I study His Word, the surer I can be of recognizing the cadences of His voice.

—JOHN SHERRILL

PRAY: *Father, train my ears to hear Your voice.*

DO: Practice listening for birdcalls. How many different ones can you hear in five minutes? Practice listening that intently for the voice of God.

WHEN YOU'RE UPSET
WITH A FAMILY MEMBER

◄○►

READ: *Being reviled, we bless. . . .*

—1 CORINTHIANS 4:12

REFLECT: When our grandchildren were small, our visits to their home always brought a chorus of "Can we come and stay the night?" We loved having them.

One night when saying her prayers, Marinell, the youngest, said, "God bless Mama, God bless Daddy, God bless Paul Mark, God bless Grandma and Grandpa."

"You left out Stokes," I told her.

"I'm not going to 'God bless' him."

Surprised, I asked, "Why not?"

"Because he wouldn't let me have the marbles."

"But we must forgive our enemies," I reminded her.

"He's not my enemy, he's my brother," she said firmly.

"Then *I'll* ask God to bless him," I told her. "God bless all brothers."

As I tucked her in, I heard a small voice murmur, "God bless Stokes."

Were I to look at all people as my *brothers* and no one as my *enemies*, there would be far more thanks and blessings in my prayers.

—ZONA B. DAVIS

PRAY: *I want to be like a child, Lord, who lets go of grievances so easily.*

DO: "God bless" that family member you're upset with.

When you're wondering if you've heard God's leading

◄◦►

READ: *Blessed is the man who listens to me. . . .*

—PROVERBS 8:34

REFLECT: I'm sometimes suspicious of people who claim their actions are led by the Spirit. Then one day I had my experience with feeling led. I was leaving the house to go to a funeral when I heard a quiet voice saying, "Take some bread." I hesitated, but it was strong enough that I found myself wrapping one of five freshly baked loaves in foil and leaving with it. I still felt odd about it, and by the time I arrived had decided to leave the bundle on the car seat.

I forgot about it until the deceased's family got ready to leave the funeral home and I overheard the daughter say, "I'm sorry, Dad, but we have to stop by the store for bread on the way home." I realized the impact of her simple statement and hurried to the car. The amazement on her face changed to radiant when I said quietly, "The Spirit led me."

—VICKI SCHAD

PRAY: *Wrap Your arms around those who are mourning today, Lord.*

DO: Follow through on the next nudge you have that you suspect could be God's leading.

WHEN YOU'RE WONDERING WHAT'S AROUND THE CORNER

◄○►

READ: *"Where have you made a raid today?"*

—I SAMUEL 27:10

REFLECT: My favorite work of painter Bob Judah was a collection of roads he'd known and loved. Bob's friendship with the roads dated back over seventy years: paved, dirt, rocky, slick, obscure, open—they led me through an adventure of seasons and locations. No figures on the roads, not even animals. Yet Bob painted life, emotion and something almost spiritual into the pictures.

"Bob," I said to him once, "all the roads have a curve in them! They beckon me. Seems like there's something good waiting for me around the curve."

Bob looked pleased. "That's right. When you get discouraged about the future, start believing that God really has something for you—just around the next curve—and keep moving toward it."

Now, when I get disheartened, I try to create a road in my mind, reminding myself that just around the next curve is something good—something from God.

—MARION BOND WEST

PRAY: *Forgive me, God, for fearing what's around the next bend in the road. Whatever is waiting there, I know it's good.*

DO: Find your own road picture and anticipate what God has for you next.

WHEN YOU'RE WORRIED

◄○►

READ: *The fear of man brings a snare, But whoever trusts in the Lord shall be safe.*

—PROVERBS 29:25

REFLECT: I've been guilty of envisioning all kinds of dark possibilities for my family and me, worries that greatly disturb my peace of mind. What if our son were injured on his construction job? What if our daughter's car broke down in the middle of nowhere on her way back to college? What if . . .

Then one day I heard a story about St. Francis of Assisi that made me think. It seems that the saint was hoeing beans in a garden near the monastery when another monk rushed up and announced excitedly that the world would end in the next fifteen minutes.

"What are you going to do?" cried the monk.

"I'm going to finish hoeing these beans," replied St. Francis.

What a simple, common sense way of dealing with unsubstantiated worries. Instead of distressing himself over something that might not come to pass, he put his faith in the Lord and got on with his everyday tasks.

—MADGE HARRAH

PRAY: *I'm sorry for worrying, God. I'll just go about my business now, rather than distress myself over something that may never come to pass.*

DO: Do exactly what you just prayed.

WHEN YOU'VE
BECOME BITTER

◄○►

READ: *Let all bitterness, wrath, anger, clamor, and evil speaking be put away from you, with all malice.*

—EPHESIANS 4:31

REFLECT: In grade school, our son Eric was diagnosed as "learning disabled." Although his IQ tested high, he still had trouble reading and handling math skills. Few teachers had been trained to work with children like Eric, and so my husband and I spent several years trying to share with the public school system all that we were learning from psychologists and parent support groups.

There were times, however, when I got so frustrated that I became a yelling, table-pounding hothead. After I'd related one of those scenes to a friend she said, "Look, you can let your problems make you *bitter* or *better*. Which do you choose?"

A good question. Answering it took a number of prayers, but I had to admit that bitterness would do no good. I did return to the fray with the school system, but this time I took a positive approach strengthened by the Lord's support, which helped me reach through to those involved.

—MADGE HARRAH

PRAY: *Lord Jesus, You were misunderstood and mistreated, but it didn't make You bitter. With Your help, I choose to follow Your example, Lord.*

DO: Search your heart for any area of bitterness and turn it into *better*.

When you've been blind to your surroundings

---◄◦►---

READ: *The hearing ear and the seeing eye, The Lord has made them both.*

—PROVERBS 20:12

REFLECT: Helen Keller once asked a friend who had just returned from a walk in the woods what she had seen. "Nothing in particular," her friend replied. Miss Keller said, "I might have been incredulous had I not long ago become convinced that the seeing see little."

The words challenged me: *What have I seen today?* I didn't have to think hard. I was seeing pitifully little. *Lord,* I prayed silently, *open my eyes.*

Then I saw, *really* saw, the colorful wooden cross from Guatemala hanging on my bulletin board that reminded me of Christ's presence.

Later, when talking with a co-worker, I noticed her downcast eyes. *I'll be a blessing to her today,* I resolved. Over lunch she shared her concerns and then we prayed together.

Look around you right now! Notice the things and people that surround you. Perhaps you, too, will discover something—or someone—beautiful, right where you are.

—ROBIN WHITE GOODE

PRAY: *Open my eyes, Lord, to see, really see, the people and things around me.*

DO: Take a picture of a new discovery since you've become newly observant.

WHEN YOU'VE
BEEN CORRECTED

READ: *No discipline seems pleasant at the time, but painful. Later on, however, it produces a harvest of righteousness and peace....*

—HEBREWS 12:11 (NIV)

REFLECT: I'll never forget the day I got a knock in the teeth from my mother—verbally, that is. It happened during a long-distance phone conversation. I had interrupted her three times. She snapped, "Will you be quiet! You know, your brother couldn't slide a word in the last time you called him. He said to me, 'Carol is so rude. She never lets anyone else talk.'"

Ooh, that smarted. Hanging up in a daze, I thought, *I'm not like that . . . am I?* I took a closer look. Wasn't I nicknamed "Mighty Mouth" in junior high? Didn't my high school English teacher often quote "Silence is golden" to me?

My mother and brother were right. I was cruising through conversations even on a red light. It was time someone stopped me. I reached for the phone to make a couple of thank-you calls.

—CAROL KNAPP

PRAY: *Father, thank You for stopping me in my tracks and changing my path.*

DO: Make a call or two to right a wrong you've done.

When you've
been criticized

READ: *The words of the wise are like goads. . . .*
  —ECCLESIASTES 12:11

REFLECT: I joined a health club, thinking that exercise might help my back problems. One day while luxuriating in the sauna, I recognized my doctor. When he asked about my back, I replied that exercise seemed to be helping a little.

"Good," he said. "But stand up straight. You slouch too much."

Slouch! I was already annoyed by his professional failure as far as my back was concerned—and now this criticism cut like a knife. But I must admit that I instinctively straightened up. And every time after that when I thought of his words, I automatically stood tall. And the taller I stood, the better I felt.

I guess that sometimes we just need to be pushed hard for our own good—and then be big enough to bless the person who cares enough to do it and humble enough to take the advice.
  —SAM JUSTICE

PRAY: *Lord, I can give constructive criticism much easier than I can take it. I bless those in my life who care enough to give it out.*

DO: Listen for God in the criticisms of others and bless them instead of getting angry.

WHEN YOU'VE BEEN
HOLDING A GRUDGE

◄O►

READ: *"Lord, how often shall my brother sin against me, and I forgive him?*

—MATTHEW 18:21

REFLECT: I once heard a little story that impelled me to take some action that I should have taken much sooner. According to the story, Clara Barton, the founder of the nursing profession, never was known to hold resentment against anyone. One time a friend reminded her of a cruel thing that had happened to her some years previous, but Clara seemed not to recall the incident. The friend asked, "Don't you remember the wrong that was done to you?"

"No," said Clara. "I distinctly remember forgetting that."

I pondered that story for a while. Then I called up a former friend who I thought had done me an unkindness, told him that I was ashamed of harboring a grudge and asked him if he'd care to have lunch and resume our old friendship. There was surprise and gladness in his voice when he said he certainly would.

—GLENN KITTLER

PRAY: *Remind me, Father, to forget unkindnesses done to me.*

DO: Make that phone call to end a grudge and restore a relationship.

WHEN YOU'VE BEEN
SURPRISED BY A BLESSING

---◄O►---

READ: *Philip said to Him, "Lord, show us the Father, and it is sufficient for us."*

—JOHN 14:8

REFLECT: Before my husband Jim was discharged from the Army, a friend invited me over for coffee. "We'll chat, just the two of us," she said. But soon after I arrived, her doorbell rang. Two other women I knew walked in. Gradually a dozen or so women finally settled into the living room. I sat there bewildered.

My friend looked at me and said in a rather exasperated voice, "Terry, don't you know what's going on? It's a surprise going-away coffee for you," she laughed.

I buried my face in my hands. How could I have been so naive?

How many times have I been slow to grasp that I've been in God's Presence? Like when my neighbor Pat brought dog biscuits to feed the stray or when my friend Nancy drove my daughter Mandy to school because I was sick. Sometimes it's only in retrospect that I see God's Presence in the caring of others.

—TERRY HELWIG

PRAY: *Lord, I'm often slow to see Your blessings. Open my eyes to Your gifts of love that always surround me.*

DO: Surprise someone with love today with a kind deed, a gift, a word of encouragement.

WHEN YOU'VE BEEN SURPRISED BY GOSSIP

READ: *Even so the tongue is a little member and boasts great things, See how great a forest a little fire kindles!*

—JAMES 3:5

REFLECT: I introduced Charity, one of my best friends, to the acquaintance sitting next to me at a college football game. They had gone through school together but hadn't kept in touch. After Charity went up to her seat, the man turned to me and said, "You know, I was in law school when her father was sent to prison for embezzlement."

Seeing the startled look on my face, he quickly changed the subject. But the afternoon was ruined for me. We had lived in this town for ten years and no one had ever said a word about such a thing. I knew Charity's father well and had always had a good relationship with the family.

I don't remember anything about the football game that day, but I do remember that I vowed to make every statement pass through three gates:

Gate one: Is it true?
Gate two: Will it hurt anyone?
Gate three: Will it help anyone?

—DOROTHY SHELLENBERGER

PRAY: *Lord, help me forget the gossip I've heard and believe only what I know to be true.*

DO: Vow to have every statement you make pass through the three gates listed above.

WHEN YOU'VE EXPERIENCED AN UNEXPECTED KINDNESS

◄◦►

READ: *Has God not chosen the poor of this world to be rich in faith and heirs of the kingdom which He promised to those who love Him?*

—JAMES 2:5

REFLECT: The elderly cab driver not only stopped for me that blizzardy day, but sprang out to help with my groceries. "Thank heaven you came along," I said. "I was getting desperate. I guess a lot of drivers just stay home on a day like this."

"Not me." His voice was cheerful. "I like to drive in the storm where I know I'm needed. It makes me rich."

"Rich?" The cab was worn, the upholstery peeling.

"Yes, rich," he insisted calmly "There were twelve of us children and we were very poor, only our mother taught us to be rich. 'There are plenty of people that can't see—you can use your eyes to help them. Some people have to be carried. You be the person that learns to do the carrying. That's what makes you rich.'"

As years went by, I discovered something more: Strength used to help others is strength and riches.

—MARJORIE HOLMES

PRAY: *Thank You, Father, for giving me so much with which to help others who have less.*

DO: Be intentional about helping the helpless today.

WHEN YOU'VE HAD
A DISAGREEMENT
WITH A FRIEND

<o>

READ: *For the word of God is living and powerful, and sharper than any two-edged sword . . . and is a discerner of the thoughts and intents of the heart.*

—HEBREWS 4:12

REFLECT: I'm normally a get-along-with-everybody person, but that self-image suddenly changed one day when my best friend and I had a sharp disagreement. I told her I was right. And why I was right. And that others agreed I was right.

Later I learned that indeed I was right. The trouble was, I didn't feel any better about it. In fact, I felt worse.

Lord, I prayed, *You knew I was right. So why do I feel terrible now?*

I stewed about it for days, then I finally sensed His answer: *"Yes, you were right. It was your attitude that was wrong."*

I might have won a little victory in a difference of opinion, but I might have lost a dear friend.

With that, I apologized. "My attitude was so wrong. Please forgive me."

She did. Our warm relationship was restored.

I no longer remember what the argument itself was about. It had seemed so important, so all-absorbing at one time. Not now.

—ISABEL WOLSELEY

PRAY: *Thank You, Father, for reminding me that letting people know I love them is far more important than letting them know I'm right.*

DO: Apologize to a friend for your part in a difference of opinion that damaged your relationship.

WHEN YOU'VE
JUDGED OTHERS

◄○►

READ: *"Do not judge, and you will not be judged."*

—LUKE 6:37

REFLECT: I left church that sunshiny morning feeling a bit smug. The sermon had been a stern attack on the "big three" —alcohol, cigarettes and drugs. I could be smug. I was a nonsmoker and nondrinker who had never touched hard drugs, and I felt a benign kind of pity for those who had.

And then the Lord, as He so frequently does, popped my balloon. He reminded me in clear "instant replays" of times when I had been "drunk" with the pride of overcoming these temptations; "smoking" over the way I'd been slighted by a busy salesclerk; had "hangovers" of depression when life didn't give me what I thought I deserved.

A quiet voice seemed to say, "Shall I go on?"

Contritely I replied, "No, thanks. I got the message."

And the message was that I could do as much damage to myself by pride, greed, envy, hatred and fear as I could by consuming harmful substances.

—DORIS SWEHLA

PRAY: *I get the message, Lord. Nothing is more damaging than my pride—to myself, to others and to my relationship with You. Forgive me, please, Lord, for judging others.*

DO: Do what you can to help a friend struggling with addiction.

WHEN YOU'VE
LOST A FRIEND

◄○►

READ: *I will not leave you orphans; I will come to you.*

—JOHN 14:18

REFLECT: As a young career woman, I shared my first Manhattan apartment with my friend Neva. We borrowed each other's clothes and jewelry. We sat up far into the night, discussing our dreams. We were very close. Then, after three years, Neva met Victor. They fell in love and got married. I was the maid of honor at their wedding.

That evening, after returning to the all-too-quiet apartment, I realized that life for me would be different. In the silence of the room, an overpowering feeling of loneliness enveloped me.

"Dear Lord," I prayed, "please help me." And He did. Suddenly I recalled His promise to send the Comforter. *He will be my Companion*, I said to myself. And with that thought, the feeling of loneliness left.

As the Comforter came to Jesus' disciples so long ago in their moment of need, He also came to me in mine. And He has been with me ever since. —ELEANOR SASS

PRAY: *Father God, please help me. Take this loneliness from me and be my Companion.*

DO: Be sensitive to your friends' feelings when your life takes a turn in another direction away from them.

WHEN YOU'VE LOST
A LOVED ONE

<o>

READ: *Give them beauty for ashes, The oil of joy for mourning, the garment of praise for the spirit of heaviness.*

—ISAIAH 61:3

REFLECT: On a trip, my husband and I stopped in a small beach community. As we turned onto the main street of the town, I recalled a week I'd once spent there with Mary. She was the closest friend I'd ever had. She cared about my joys and my problems, and would encourage me to seek the Lord.

The memories were precious, yet painful, because Mary had died of a brain tumor. Even though I knew she was with Jesus, there was a heaviness in my heart that would not go away.

Driving home, I said wistfully to my husband, "I wonder if I'll ever have another friend like Mary."

"Honey," he said gently, "you can *be* a friend like Mary."

Almost immediately those words began to dissolve the ache in my heart. Our friendship did not have to end. It could touch more lives because Mary's love and caring had become a part of me.

—LORRAINE DAVIES

PRAY: *Jesus, help me be a friend who cares about others' joys and problems.*

DO: Express your love and concern for a new friend today.

WHEN YOU'VE LOST
SOMETHING VALUABLE

◄○►

READ: *A time to gain, And a time to lose; A time to keep, And a time to throw away....*

—ECCLESIASTES 3:6

REFLECT: I once lost a valuable coral-and-silver bracelet at a concert in a large auditorium. I went back the next day and searched the auditorium and the parking lot, but I didn't find the bracelet, nor did it ever turn up at the lost-and-found.

When I bemoaned my loss to my friend Elsie, she said, "Nothing is ever lost. You don't have the bracelet anymore, but somebody does. Bless that person and let the bracelet go."

Following her suggestion, I thought of the bracelet on another woman's arm and said a short prayer: "Lord, let that woman wear the bracelet in health and joy." A weight lifted from my heart, replaced by a feeling of peace.

—MADGE HARRAH

PRAY: *Thank You, Father, for the wisdom of friends. Once again, help me to gracefully let go of the things I can't control.*

DO: Pray for God to help you find your lost valuable, but also ask Him to let you know when it's time to let it go.

WHEN YOU'VE MADE
A COSTLY MISTAKE

---◄○►---

READ: *To everything there is a season, A time for every purpose under heaven.... A time to weep, And a time to laugh; a time to mourn, And a time to dance....*

—ECCLESIASTES 3:1–4

REFLECT: My wife Beth and I were rushing to catch a plane. As I drove madly toward the airport, a torrential rain beat down.

Careering into the airport parking lot, I parked in the first available space. Grabbing our luggage, we sprinted to the ticket counter and then the gate. Two minutes later and we would have missed our flight.

Five weeks later, we returned. As we walked through the long-term parking area, I could not find my car. Looking intently at my parking ticket stub, I discovered my mistake: I had parked in the short-term lot. The fee was seven dollars a day; my blunder had cost me two hundred and fifty-two dollars!

As I drove slowly home, I fumed, ready to explode. Suddenly, Beth started giggling and then burst into laughter. And before I knew it, I was laughing too. I could hear the voice of my mother repeating her favorite maxim: "Well, you can laugh or you can cry!"

—SCOTT WALKER

PRAY: *Lord God, make me able to laugh at my mistakes, even the expensive ones.*

DO: Think of your mistake in light of eternity. How bad is it, really?

WHEN YOU'VE MISJUDGED A FRIEND

◄○►

READ: *Though I speak with the tongues of men and of angels, but have not love, I have become sounding brass or a clanging cymbal.*

—1 CORINTHIANS 13:1

REFLECT: I guess I'd have to say I was a "Christian snob" that year. I had a collection of friends and didn't feel a need for some on the perimeter, like my husband's old college pal Joe, the partygoer. Even though he wasn't like that anymore, I couldn't see any reason to be more than politely friendly to "that type." After all, I had my Christian friends to turn to in hard times.

And then hard times came. The miscarriage wasn't physically difficult, but emotionally it was. My friends stood by me, but my heart ached at the pat phrases most gave as comfort. I would thank them for being there, but alone I would cry, craving something although I wasn't sure what.

That "something" arrived in the mail. I only got one. I still have it.

My beautiful blue sympathy card. Inside was written, "I am so sorry."

It was from Joe.

—KATHIE KANIA

PRAY: *I'm sorry, God, for being judgmental. Help my heart to be open to all people whether I like them or not.*

DO: Send a note of encouragement to someone who would expect it least from you.

WHEN YOU'VE OVERESTIMATED YOUR ABILITIES

◄○►

READ: *You caused judgment to be heard from heaven; The earth feared and was still....*

—PSALM 76:8

REFLECT: I have a tendency to think I can do anything, even in areas where my skills and knowledge are limited. Then once, while renovating a house (one of those areas where I'm really limited), I fell off a ladder and broke some ribs and a wrist. For days I was completely undone by my immobility. So when a dear friend invited me to her home in the country, I jumped at the chance to get my mind off my fractured bones.

One morning I wakened to a quiet world covered with snow and ice. Nothing moved. Everything was beautiful and caught in an awesome, perfect stillness.

It seemed God was trying to say through the beautiful snowfall, "Be still and know that I am God." Although God may want me to work and be active at other times, *now* it was time for stillness. To heal my spirit, to stop, to contemplate, to *know*—that He is God. —SAMANTHA MCGARRITY

PRAY: *Father, thank You for quieting my soul and healing my body.*

DO: Find a new place and a new way to rest in God today.

WHEN YOU'VE STOPPED GOING TO CHURCH

---◀◉▶---

READ: *Let us not give up meeting together. . . .*

—HEBREWS 10:25 (NIV)

REFLECT: My son found a cardinal with a broken leg. We splint the poor leg and named our cardinal Flame. He lived in a big cage on a sheltered porch. Flame seemed happy and sang for us beautifully. A few sparrows chattered about his cage to keep him company.

"What's the matter with Flame?" I asked a few weeks later. "All he does is chirp. What happened to his lovely song?"

"I think he's forgotten his song," my husband declared. "He only hears sparrows now. He needs to be with cardinals to sing his true song."

We decided to let Flame fly away.

It's not just birds. We're all affected by the people we're with. Surely the joy, love and faith of every member of our Christian church is inspired by others.

—LUCILLE CAMPBELL

PRAY: *I praise You, God, for being the song in my heart and for others who help me sing it.*

DO: If you've stopped going to church, try to find one that sings your kind of song.

WHEN YOU'VE SUFFERED
A CAREER SETBACK

◄◊►

READ: *For you have need of endurance, so that after you have done the will of God, you may receive the promise.*

—HEBREWS 10:36

REFLECT: During a career setback that made me want to give up, my friend LeAnn told me about her experience in 4-H club. A city-bred girl trying to compete with ranch kids, she'd spent all her free time grooming and training her chestnut calf Jessica. Still, they placed last at the spring showing. After leading her calf out of the ring, she ran into her father's arms and sobbed, "Oh, Daddy. Jessica and I just aren't good enough. I'm going to quit showing."

"Well, that's up to you," said her father. "But remember one thing. You're only a loser if you quit praying and trying."

Several months of intensive work and many prayers later, LeAnn and Jessica went on to capture two purple ribbons at the state showing, the largest 4-H show in the world.

If you're feeling discouraged today, remember that you're only a loser if you quit praying and trying.

—MARILYN MORGAN KING

PRAY: *No one had it harder than You, Lord Jesus, yet You never gave up. Help me to keep trying, no matter how hard it is.*

DO: Make your own purple ribbon to say to a friend that you think he/she is a winner.

WHEN YOU'VE TURNED YOUR BACK ON GOD

---◀○▶---

READ: *The word is very near you, in your mouth and in your heart, that you may do it.*

—DEUTERONOMY 30:14

REFLECT: I was one of those "Bible whiz kids" who memorized so much Scripture that I won every contest I entered. When I went to medical school, though, I turned my back on God. Faith in God didn't make sense in a world where innocent children died of diseases they were too young to pronounce. By the time I became a doctor, I had put away the Bible, and my feelings.

One day I had no words of consolation to offer a family, so I sat quietly with them at the bedside of their dying child. It was in that quiet of my heart that I heard it—the Word— in my heart, so near: *Let not your heart be troubled. . . . My peace I give to you; not as the world gives . . . (John 14:1, 27, NKJV).* God's Word was still there in my heart, stored up for the time when I could hear with more than my ears.

—DIANE KOMP

PRAY: *Father, today I would love to hear a faith-renewing word from You.*

DO: Search your memory, and your Bible, for a Scripture that will help renew your faith.

When you've witnessed unkindness

READ: *Now abide faith, hope, love, these three; but the greatest of these is love.*

—1 CORINTHIANS 13:13

REFLECT: During my student years, I worked as an orderly in large city hospital. One man in a four-bed ward was very sick. He'd had a stroke and was only semiconscious. Two women were with him through the course of my shift. One was the head nurse. The other was a beginning student.

The head nurse was abrupt and impatient, and not at all thorough. But the student nurse was kind and gentle, and never satisfied with a halfway job. Just before my shift was over, one of the men summed up what we all felt. He said, "That one is in charge—but the other's a nurse."

Through the years I've applied his observation to other situations. Here's a man with children—but there's a father. Here's a person assigned to a classroom—but there's a teacher. What makes the difference? It's patience and kindness—it's love.

—JOHN MARTIN MASON

PRAY: *Whatever You've created me to do, Father, remind me to do it with love.*

DO: Analyze yourself. Are you doing your job with love, or just doing your job?

WHEN YOU'VE YELLED AT YOUR KIDS

———◄◐►———

READ: *"Whoever would love life and see good days must keep his tongue from evil. . . .*

—1 PETER 3:10 (NIV)

REFLECT: A national newspaper once noted that the Lord's Prayer contained fifty-six words, the Twenty-third Psalm 118 words, the Gettysburg Address 226 words and the Ten Commandments 297 words . . . while the US Department of Agriculture directive on pricing cabbage weighed in at 15,629 words.

The Ag Department directive reminds me of the way I sometimes shout at my children when I think they need it. First I rant and rave, then I rave and rant, usually repeating myself three or four times. Then, once again for emphasis but in a quieter, more adult tone I recap my sentiments with a "Do you understand?"

Of course they understand. They understood completely at the end of the first fifteen seconds. Was my fifteen-minute tirade really necessary? Of course not. One simple, calm "Mother Knows Best" directive would have done it . . . with a possible silent fifty-six word "Our Father" tucked at the end.

—PATRICIA LORENZ

PRAY: *Lord, give me the wisdom to stop talking, especially to stop yelling at my kids, when my point has been made.*

DO: Apologize to your child(ren) for yelling and express your commitment to correct them more gently.

When your attitude
is negative

———————<o>———————

READ: *Refuse the evil, and choose the good.*

—ISAIAH 7:15

REFLECT: "Can you believe this family?" I asked our friend Rich as I put down the newspaper I'd been reading. We were chaperoning a church outing, waiting for the kids to get into the van.

I pointed to the headlines of the paper that announced yet another lawsuit pitting parents against son in a malicious battle over an inheritance.

"Oh," Rich said, "to be honest, I just don't have the time to read stories like that. There are more than enough positive things to keep me occupied."

I can't tell you how many times I've recalled Rich's response to that local scandal. In his small effort, I see possibilities for improving my own choices.

When others are saying mean things about someone, when a friend is being critical in public, when a family member is being pessimistic, I can refuse to participate. I can say something constructive. I can turn the mood positive.

It sure does feel good to choose good. Why would I want to live any other way?

—PAM KIDD

PRAY: *Give me courage, God, to choose good, especially when others I'm with are not.*

DO: Apologize for any negativity you've spread around to others.

WHEN YOUR CHILD
IS A PERFECTIONIST

◄○►

READ: *"My grace is sufficient for you," for My strength is made perfect in weakness.*

—2 CORINTHIANS 12:9

REFLECT: At eight, Elizabeth is making real progress with her violin, and she's a fine student in her school subjects too. But she's also a perfectionist. If it's not perfect, she thinks, it's no good. And what's worse, neither is she. "Honey," I said, "You can't expect to play the piece perfectly all at once. Work on it a few measures at a time."

"I never want to play the violin again!" she said, stamping her foot.

I know how Elizabeth feels. Remembering the gaffes I've committed over the years still causes me embarrassment. I don't want to admit that I'm not a perfect Christian, a perfect husband, a perfect father. And I certainly don't want to admit that the source of my perfectionism is pride.

It's not easy for me to remember that what really matters is to grow in love, and for that, Christ's grace is sufficient. It's a hard lesson to explain to an eight-year-old, but it's a lesson I pray Elizabeth will learn. —ANDREW ATTAWAY

PRAY: *Lord, in my weakness You perfect Your strength. Help me to give myself—imperfections and all—to You.*

DO: Memorize 2 Corinthians 12:9 with your child(ren).

WHEN YOUR CHILD IS IN DANGER

◄○►

READ: *But the Lord is faithful, who will establish you and guard you from the evil one.*

—2 THESSALONIANS 3:3

REFLECT: Sometimes my friend Ursula is worried to tears about her oldest son, a Navy SEAL who has just been assigned to an assault team. Whatever that actually is, the title alone was enough to sicken her.

In the summer of 1999 Ursala's husband Jim was diagnosed with multiple myeloma. During his bone marrow transplant, chemotherapy and radiation treatments, her father died when his bleeding ulcer hemorrhaged. Then Jim's cancer ushered him into Jesus' presence forever.

Ursula is walking through her grief one day (or one minute) at a time with God and friends who love and pray for her. Still, some days are really hard, like when her son tells her he's going to be on a SEAL assault team.

So, our ladies' prayer group formed our own assault team. We deployed a squad of angels to surround and protect her son. We asked God to send Christians into his life to relentlessly pursue him. Finally, we asked the Holy Spirit to assault him with God's love until he surrenders his heart utterly and completely to Jesus. —LUCILE ALLEN

PRAY: *I pray for soldiers everywhere today, Lord. Send Your angels to protect them and give their mothers peace.*

DO: Gather a group of friends to pray for a loved one (or the child of a loved one) in danger.

WHEN YOUR CHILD(REN) ASK HARD QUESTIONS ABOUT FAITH

<o>

READ: *God will wipe every tear from their eyes. . . .*

—REVELATION 21:4

REFLECT: While putting the kids to bed, I stopped to pray for a friend in the midst of a difficult labor and delivery. Moments after I asked God to keep Mary Ellen and her baby safe and healthy, my daughter Elizabeth wanted to know what could go wrong. I groaned.

Elizabeth grasped for the first time that some children die as infants and that others are born with physical problems. Sorrow and a sense of injustice fell deep in her heart. "It doesn't seem fair!" she sobbed. "Why does God allow that?"

Oh dear. I talked to my grief-stricken child as best I could, knowing that even the most profound words probably meant far less than the reassurance of my arms wrapped around her.

I gave her a kiss and left her to pray her way to sleep. I prayed for my daughter while I washed the dishes. Then I prayed for all those struggling to understand the ways of God.

—JULIE ATTAWAY

PRAY: *Lord Jesus, You answered all our unanswerable questions on the cross. Let my heart rest there with You when I wrestle with hard questions of faith.*

DO: Show your child(ren) some hard Scriptures and how men and women of faith drew strength from God.

WHEN YOUR CHILD(REN) BEGIN TO PULL AWAY

READ: *God is our refuge and strength.... Therefore we will not fear, though the earth give way....*

—PSALM 46:1–2 (NIV)

REFLECT: One day after school Kendall and I stopped at a department store. Though she was ten, she was the baby of the family. As we crossed the parking lot, I instinctively reached down for her hand. Instinctively, she pulled it away.

"I'll hold your hand at home and at church, but not here," she shyly smiled up at me. The sentence was short but the message was weighty: Kendall was growing up.

Always, we face changes that are part of God's plan. We can resist and hold on tightly. Or we can cooperate and hold on lightly, gathering up the blessings from our past and moving forward.

—CAROL KUYKENDALL

PRAY: *Father, as my child(ren) let go of my hand, I pray they take hold of Yours.*

DO: Pray with your child(ren), releasing them into God's hands.

WHEN YOUR CHILDREN ARE AT ODDS WITH EACH OTHER

◄○►

READ: *You, who once were alienated . . . now He has reconciled.*

—COLOSSIANS 1:21

REFLECT: My sons Paul and John had a falling out that has kept them at odds for years, despite the efforts of family members and counseling. This has been the greatest sadness of my life. They were civil to each other, but the deep brotherly closeness was lost.

When Paul's wife Cheryl died, John called me and said, "Do you think it would be all right if I came to the funeral? I'd like to be there for Paul." I was touched, though a bit uneasy. But I said he should come.

Paul and Cheryl's brother Steve had suggested five pallbearers. When I told Paul about John's call, he responded enthusiastically, "I'd love to see John! Can he be a pallbearer?"

John arrived, and Paul thanked him for coming. Then a miracle happened. Each apologized to the other. They accepted each other's forgiveness and hugged and wiped the tears from their eyes. I cried too—tears of joy and thanksgiving. My sons were brothers again!

—MARILYN MORGAN KING

PRAY: *I pray for my children, Lord, that You would intervene, and give them the gift of forgiveness and a restored relationship.*

DO: Continue to pray for the miracle of restored friendship between your children.

WHEN YOUR CHILDREN ARE TOO BUSY

———————————◄○►———————————

READ: *Surely I have calmed and quieted my soul. . . .*

—PSALM 131:2

REFLECT: I was rushing down the rain-swept freeway with my son Julian in tow when I noticed that he was particularly quiet in the backseat. I looked at him and saw him staring out the window.

"Look, Julian," I said, "you can play games on my cell phone!"

"Okay," he said without much enthusiasm.

Later, massive storm clouds were still unleashing torrents of rain, while three spectacular bolts of sun broke through the clouds.

I looked back at Julian staring intently at the cell phone's tiny screen. *Why couldn't I have just left him to enjoy the beauty around him?*

It occurred to me that none of us has time to simply sit and reflect. Besides work and school, there are soccer, swim lessons, working out, church activities. . . . and the entertainment that fills up whatever time's left over, like the TV, computer games, even games on the phone.

We've lost the quiet spaces that God can fill up with the beauty of a storm.

—DAVE FRANCO

PRAY: *Lord, please teach me and teach my children to appreciate quietness and Your beauty.*

DO: Sit outside and watch a storm with your children.

WHEN YOUR CHILDREN ARE UNGRATEFUL

READ: *One of them, when he saw that he was healed, returned, and with a loud voice glorified God, and fell down on his face at His feet, giving Him thanks.*

—LUKE 17:15–16

REFLECT: My sister-in-law Eve was a difficult adolescent. Willful, bright and independent, she could make life very trying for her mother. Yet her mother never gave up. She just gave. Eve grew up and married, and then, one year when she was in her thirties, she hosted a difficult thirteen-year-old for a summer. At the end of it, she phoned her mother, and, for the first time in two decades, thanked her: "I never realized how much you gave me and how hard it must have been."

As a father, I now see many things my parents gave me. What burdens did they bear, what sacrifices did they make? I'll never be able to count them all. But as a child, I received—blissfully ignorant of the gifts. It makes me think of all the gifts I receive from God every day. How often do I say, "Thank You"?

—RICK HAMLIN

PRAY: *Father, I'm so grateful that You never quit giving to me because of my ingratitude. I'm thankful for all You do for me.*

DO: Never give up on your difficult child(ren). Just give.

WHEN YOUR CHILDREN
ARE UPSET WITH YOU

◄○►

READ: *Be imitators of God as dear children. And walk in love. . . .*

— EPHESIANS 5:1–2

REFLECT: A college professor I heard of once told his little daughter to do something. She announced that she would not. He sent the child to her room immediately.

Later that day, when he went to sit down in his chair, he found a note on the seat. It said, "I hate Daddy."

Angrily he called his wife and showed her the note. "I'm going to teach her a thing or two," he declared.

"Don't do anything rash," his wife told him. "Think about it."

With difficulty, he took her advice. He thought about it. Finally, he wrote a note under hers, "Daddy loves you," and placed it on her pillow.

A few moments after his daughter discovered his note, she came to him with the same piece of paper. Written on the back of it were these words: "I love Daddy too."

— ZONA B. DAVIS

PRAY: *Father, even when I'm upset with You and don't want to obey You, I love You.*

DO: Write a love note to your child(ren).

WHEN YOUR CHILDREN FACE REJECTION

———◄○►———

READ: *With joy you will draw water From the wells of salvation.*

—ISAIAH 12:3

REFLECT: A group of children, mine and the neighbor's, were playing in the next room when I heard them shout at my four-year-old daughter, "Go away, we don't want you with us!"

She came running and I held her as she sobbed. Finally, in a quivering voice, she asked, "Does God cry, Mommy?"

I thought of how from the dawn of creation God has been aching over people who reject Him. I remembered, too, a verse in the Bible that had never meant much to me, except that I knew it was the shortest one.

"Jesus wept" (John 11:35).

Our God has shed tears! He's known rejection, physical and emotional pain, temptation . . . anything we go through. He knows what it's like.

"Yes, Sanna. God cries too."

"Good," she answered and jumped down from my lap, ready to face life again.

I find life easier to face with that knowledge too.

—SHARI SMYTH

PRAY: *Jesus, I pray You will turn the rejection in my children's lives to compassion for others who are experiencing rejection.*

DO: Include a newcomer in a family activity.

WHEN YOUR COMPUTER IS DOWN

◄◦►

READ: *I hope to come to you and speak face to face, that our joy may be full.*

—2 JOHN 12

REFLECT: "E-mail's down!" I must have heard that message three times between the elevator and my desk. I could only sigh as I glanced at my barren computer screen.

By three o'clock the tech department no longer answered its phones. I stalked down the hall to deliver a manuscript to an editor to whom I would have normally e-mailed my suggestions. "Oh, who's that?" I asked, noticing a snapshot of a newborn on her bulletin board.

"That's my nephew!" she said proudly.

"Wow, your first one?"

"Yep."

"Congratulations. By the way, nice work on this story."

"Thanks."

It struck me how good it felt just to exchange a few words. Yes, a lot of our technology shrinks the world and makes it easier for us to communicate. But it can also make it easier for us *not* to communicate.

By the time I got back to my office, I hoped my computer screen was still blank. Thankfully, it was.

—EDWARD GRINNAN

PRAY: *God, don't let me forget that people are more important than technology.*

DO: Call or go see a person you normally communicate with through e-mail.

WHEN YOUR CONCEPT OF GOD IS TOO SMALL

─◄○►─

READ: *He counts the number of the stars; He calls them all by name.*

—PSALM 147:4

REFLECT: I had occasion to speak to the preschool and elementary children in our ministry's school. I asked the question, "How big is God?" Their eyes opened wide and many hands went up. One child shouted, "He is big!" Another said, "He is bigger than we are!" And yet another said, "He is bigger than this world!"

In the children's eyes, God was truly B-I-G.

When I sat down, I began to reflect on the many ways God's bigness has been reflected in my life: growing up in a poor—but loving—family; being able to attend college; creating a community ministry . . . and on and on.

The words of the psalmist came to mind: "He determines the number of the stars and calls them each by name" (Psalm 147:4).

I am thankful today for a God Who can do that kind of miracle. So now I ask you: *How big is God?* (Hint–B-I-G.)

—DOLPHUS WEARY

PRAY: *Forgive us all, Lord, for our small concept of You.*

DO: Count as many stars as you can and name a few. Consider the God Who numbered and named them all.

WHEN YOUR CONFIDENCE IS LOW

READ: *Great is your faith!*

— MATTHEW 15:28

REFLECT: Our son and his wife called "Good night!" and turned to walk off the porch. I could hear their laughter as they stepped down and started, almost at a run, toward the car. Their clasped hands, swinging between them, were more than an indication of their love. Without Mary Ann's hand, Dave, who had been born blind, would have needed his cane to find his way.

I kept thinking of the happy confidence Dave had shown running beside Mary Ann. *What utter faith in her he must have,* I thought. What complete trust in her ability and willingness to lead him so that he would not trip or fall!

Standing there in the doorway, I wondered if my life reflected that kind of faith and trust in God.

I closed the door, promising myself that I would learn from Dave. I would put my hand in God's and follow where He leads.

— LOIS T. HENDERSON

PRAY: *Walking hand in hand with You, Lord, is far greater than running ahead of You on my own.*

DO: Trade trust walks with a loved one. Take turns being led, with eyes closed, through unfamiliar territory.

WHEN YOUR FEELINGS
HAVE BEEN HURT

──◄○►──

READ: *Bear with each other and forgive whatever grievances you may have against one another. Forgive as the Lord forgave you.*

— COLOSSIANS 3:13 (NIV)

REFLECT: The onion I picked up had a soft, dark spot. Oh well, I could salvage most of it for the beef stew. While peeling back that onion, I thought of what Pastor Martin had said about forgiving old, deep hurts. "Sometimes you have to forgive in layers."

When we met, I felt sure Marie (not her real name) and I would be very close. Her little digs and hurtful comments, though, would surface now and then, and she disapproved of much about me—including some of the very things I considered my God-given assets. When I backed away from the relationship, she seemed agreeable. But it took months to peel away layers of hurt, anger and resentment.

Sometimes it takes a while, but I eventually do get to that pearly white forgiveness layer, where the offense, even upon remembrance, no longer hurts or matters.

— KATHIE KANIA

PRAY: *Father, please free my friend who's buried beneath layers of unforgiveness.*

DO: Forgive an offense, layer by layer, until the memory of it doesn't hurt anymore.

WHEN YOUR FOCUS STRAYS OFF GOD

READ: *Lift your eyes now and look from the place where you are. . . .*

—GENESIS 13:14

REFLECT: I hadn't yet turned sixteen when I learned to drive. My mother sat in the passenger's seat of our station wagon as I eased it into the street.

My eyes were hawklike, focused straight ahead. My neck and shoulder muscles were knotted. My sweaty hands gripped the wheel tightly at the two and ten o'clock positions, just the way I'd learned in Driver's Ed.

"Julie, what are you looking at?" Mom said.

"The nose of the car. I'm steering the car between the two lines. It's hard!"

"Nobody drives like that! Look way out down the road."

"How will I stay between the lines if I quit focusing on the car?"

"Trust me, you drive by looking ahead."

I shifted my glance to the horizon. Until recently, I approached life the same way: I wanted to be in control with my hard-steering technique. But now I'm learning to let go, focusing far down the road and looking only toward God.

—JULIE GARMON

PRAY: *Father, as I focus on You today, keep me on the right road.*

DO: Take your hands off the steering wheel of your life and give God control.

WHEN YOUR FRIEND IS BURDENED BY FINANCIAL PROBLEMS

<><o>>

READ: *He who has pity on the poor lends to the Lord. . . .*
                                    —PROVERBS 19:17

REFLECT: I rifled through my desk drawer looking for an eraser. I was helping my friend Joan with a loan application, and I was exasperated. "If you hadn't given your sister that money, you wouldn't be in this mess," I complained.

She tried to hide the hurt in her eyes. "My sister is more important than money," she said.

"I'm sorry I snapped at you," I said. "It's just that I hate to see you with this burden." I jumped. My hand had fallen on a piece of metal that had been knocked off my car in an accident the year before.

"What is that?" Joan asked. "Why would you keep that old thing?"

"It was supposed to be a reminder," I said.

"Of what?" she asked.

"What you just tried to tell me," I said sheepishly. "My husband and I could have been hurt in this accident. I saved it to keep me focused on what really counts. People are more important than things."
                                    —SUSAN SCHEFFLIN

PRAY: *Gracious God, would You bless my friend*
          _____ for his/her generosity
          and meet his/her financial need now.

DO: Assure your generous friend that people are, indeed, more important than things.

WHEN YOUR FRIEND
IS SEARCHING FOR PURPOSE

◄◦►

READ: *For the gifts and the calling of God are irrevocable.*

—ROMANS 11:29

REFLECT: When I was a child I was constantly told how I resembled my paternal grandmother, who died before my birth. I grew very tired of hearing it, and one day told my mother, "I don't want to be like Grandma Hall. I want to be me!"

Mother put her arm around me and said, "You are you. It doesn't matter what you look like. What's important is what you make of your life. God made you for a particular purpose. What He planned for your life, no one else can do."

I've never forgotten her words, and they have made me search for His plan for my life. Sometimes it seems so obscure that I get discouraged and frightened. I dream of doing great things, most of which elude me, and I wonder if I'll ever accomplish anything of value.

That's when I take my dreams to Him, along with my anxieties and failures, and we talk about them. And always He sends me the peace and reassurance that only He can give.

—DRUE DUKE

PRAY: *Lord, I pray for _____ that by following Your calling he/she will bring You pleasure and glory.*

DO: Assess options with your friend about how to use his/her gifts and talents.

WHEN YOUR GOALS
SEEM OUT OF REACH

◄○►

READ: *Commit your works to the Lord, And your thoughts will be established.*

—PROVERBS 16:3

REFLECT: I struggled with piano lessons, but my hands were too small to stretch an octave on the keys. I gave it up when I got old enough to protest the lessons.

One year I shared a monastery guesthouse with a young man named Douglas who wanted to be a jazz trumpeter. He moved in with hundreds of CDs and a shiny trumpet. I was eager to hear him play.

Douglas practiced for four hours every day. But he played only scales, every morning, every night.

I asked him why he never played anything else. He answered, "I want to be a very good trumpet player, and I don't have a natural gift for it. So I have to work at the basics for a very long time."

Just as I hadn't had the talent, I also hadn't had the gift of working hard enough to make up for my flaws. Douglas may not get the career he wants, but it won't be for any lack of trying.

—RHODA BLECKER

PRAY: *Show me the gift You've given me, Lord, and give me the perseverance to pursue it.*

DO: Pick up a hobby you gave up on as a child and try again.

WHEN YOUR KID(S) DON'T WANT TO GO TO CHURCH

<del>──────────◄○►──────────</del>

READ: *. . . not forsaking the assembling of ourselves together. . . .*

—HEBREWS 10:25

REFLECT: Coach Pannell's ninth-grade Bible class fell silent. David had asked: "Is it okay that sometimes my parents have to make me go to church?" We sat riveted for the answer.

Coach Pannell cleared his throat and smiled. "David," he said, "do you ever not want to eat your vegetables, even though you know you're supposed to?"

"Of course," David replied.

"How about going to the dentist, even though you don't want to?"

David laughed. "I do that all the time!"

"That's just it," Coach Pannell said. "Sometimes parents know better about what's good for you, whether it's eating right, staying healthy or furthering your relationship with God. Right now church might not be as important to you as the other things on your schedule, but someday, you'll understand."

On a Sunday morning when the alarm goes off, I want to push the snooze button and go back to sleep. But by the closing strains of the final hymn, heartfelt praise has replaced the grumbles. It's a habit that began on the Sundays of my childhood.

—ASHLEY JOHNSON

PRAY: *God, thank You for parents who trained me not to hit the snooze button on Sundays.*

DO: Take a teen or two to church with you.

WHEN YOUR LOAD
FEELS TOO HEAVY

◄◌►

READ: *"The Lord is my strength and my song; he has become my salvation."*

—EXODUS 15:2

REFLECT: Coming out of the grocery store were a man and his young son. The little boy was desperately hanging onto a big bag of ice, trying to appear as if the act was effortless. His father was doing the actual carrying, holding it with true ease by its handle.

The little boy cried out, "Don't let go, Dad, don't let go!"

The father replied, "I won't, son. Is the bag too heavy? Is the ice too cold?"

"No, no, Daddy! I've got it. But don't let go!"

I know there are times when my Father says, "Teresa, is the load too heavy? Are you feeling cold and alone?"

I have to decide: Do I want to carry my problems all by myself, or will I leave them for stronger arms to bear?

—TERESA SCHANTZ

PRAY: *I'm so good at pretending to let go of my burdens, Father, but today I choose to really let go and let You carry them all.*

DO: Help a friend carry a burden, even as you encourage him/her to let go and let God carry it.

WHEN YOUR LOVED ONES MAY NOT FEEL LOVED BY YOU

━━━━━━━━━━━━━━◄○►━━━━━━━━━━━━━━

READ: *For whom the Lord loves He corrects, Just as a father the son in whom he delights.*

—PROVERBS 3:12

REFLECT: Setting the table for dinner, I was lamenting a string of minor misfortunes that had seemed to zero in on my little corner of the world. Medical bills, our dying lawn.... My list went on and on. I silently asked the Lord why I was being singled out.

One of my sons interrupted my thoughts. He looked at his place setting and said, "You don't love me as much as you love Billy, do you? You gave me the chipped plate again."

"I love you both the same," I assured him and started to exchange his plate.

"No," he said, "as long as I *know* you love me as much as Billy, it's okay."

Didn't God love me? Of course! I wasn't being singled out. "Chipped plates" just *happen* to be set at my place, and I must use my confidence in my Father's love to help overcome them.

—DORIS C. CRANDALL

PRAY: *Forgive me for accusing You, Father, of loving me less than Your other children. And thank You for showing me the ridiculousness of the very thought.*

DO: Don't assume your loved ones feel loved by you every day. Do, or say, something to make sure they do.

WHEN YOUR PLANS
AREN'T WORKING

◄○►

READ: *There are many devices in a man's heart; nevertheless the counsel of the Lord, that shall stand.*

—PROVERBS 19:21

REFLECT: Two friends launched highly successful businesses. The first runs a chain of clothing stores in the Southwest. A plaque on my friend's desk captures her philosophy: PLAN YOUR WORK. WORK YOUR PLAN.

She sets targets for each week, each month, even each decade. She's right on schedule too; her clothing empire is steadily expanding. Yet the turnover among her staff is high: No manager stays more than two or three years.

The other friend and his family own a publishing company that is the envy of the industry. On a recent visit, employees, from clerks to top executives, stopped me to describe their work with pride.

Impressed, I asked him how much time he spent planning.

"Oh, I don't plan," he said. "I listen."

How different. My second friend prays, then stays flexible, holding each decision up to God to hear what He may be saying.

We can all learn to hear God in our undertakings—but only if our own plans take second place to His.

—JOHN SHERRILL

PRAY: *Father, I submit my agenda to Your perfect plans today.*

DO: Open yourself to change—a change of methods and maybe even goals.

WHEN YOUR PRAYERS ARE ANSWERED

READ: *Pray without ceasing, in everything give thanks; for this is the will of God in Christ Jesus for you.*

—1 THESSALONIANS 5:17–18

REFLECT: I'm a person who prays a lot. But even so, I find that often I fail to recognize the answers. In fact, I recognized myself in a story a friend recently related.

It seems that a woman was searching for a parking space in a very crowded area. She circled the block a number of times before exclaiming, "Lord, please help me to find a parking space!" Sure enough, a car pulled out right in front of her, leaving her an empty spot easy to pull into. "Never mind, Lord," she added as she parked the car. "I found one myself!"

I'm going to continue to knock frequently at the Lord's door, but from now on I'll try to remember just Who opened it!

—TAMMY RIDER

PRAY: *Forgive me, Lord, for being blind to Your answers to my prayers. Help me to give glory where it's due.*

DO: Make a list of answered prayers in the past month and thank God for them.

WHEN YOUR PRAYERS SEEM UNANSWERED (I)

———◄○►———

READ: *So then faith comes by hearing, and hearing by the word of God.*

—ROMANS 10:17

REFLECT: I've been asking God for a fresh breeze of faith and, of course, I've suggested that answering a few prayers would fill my sails just fine.

"Healing Aunt Peggy's cancer would definitely remind me that nothing is too difficult for You, Lord."

"A new job for my husband—a challenging, fulfilling one—would assure me that You haven't forsaken us."

God has answered my prayer for more faith, but not in the ways I suggested. A few nights ago, as I got into bed, He slipped this thought into my head: *Faith doesn't come from answered prayers, Lucy. Faith comes from hearing the Word of God.*

I'd been letting my faith float up, down, up, down, on the waves of answered and seemingly unanswered prayers, instead of anchoring it to the unchanging Word of God. That's where He demonstrates His matchless power, His perfect timing and His commitment to unfaithful humanity. That's where a fresh breeze of faith is always blowing.

—LUCILE ALLEN

PRAY: *Thank You, Father, for Your Word, the source of all faith.*

DO: Search the Bible for a word that will increase your faith in an area it's lacking.

WHEN YOUR PRAYERS
SEEM UNANSWERED $\left(2\right)$

―◦―

READ: *"Take this staff in your hand so you can perform miraculous signs with it."*

―EXODUS 4:17 (NIV)

REFLECT: A friend told me a joke about a man named Sam who was in financial trouble and decided he'd pray to win the lottery. When the prayer wasn't answered, he added an hour to his bedtime prayer. No result. He added another hour to his morning prayer. One morning when he was beginning his second hour of prayer, he heard a Voice say, "Give me a break, Sam. Buy a ticket."

How often I expect God to intervene miraculously with no effort on my part. I put off starting assignments and then beg God to help me finish them on time. I overeat, knowing I won't sleep well, and then ask God for a good night's rest.

Of course, not all prayers are answered the way I'd like because God knows what's right for me. But before I accept this as the reason for an unanswered prayer, I'm going to remember Sam and "buy a ticket."

―BONNIE LUKES

PRAY: *Thank You, Father, that I can trust You to answer my prayers in the best way, not necessarily the way I'd like.*

DO: Ask God how to pray for a certain thing, rather than telling Him how to answer.

WHEN YOUR PRAYERS SEEM UNANSWERED (3)

————◄○►————

READ: *Now faith is the substance of things hoped for, the evidence of things not seen.*

—HEBREWS 11:1

REFLECT: It had been a season of unanswered prayers. I found myself crying out, "Are You really there, God? Can You give me one sign of hope?"

Throughout the drizzly day I waited for my sign—and received none. Later, while en route to town with my son, we passed by Stone Mountain. Every time we see it, little David says, "Look, Mama, there's the mountain we climbed." That afternoon, however, he exclaimed, "It's good we aren't going to climb Stone Mountain, Mama, because it isn't there."

"Of course it's there," I muttered automatically, then turned to look. It wasn't. The fog and mist had come down so low that not one bit of that huge mountain was visible. As I stared at the mist where I knew the mountain had to be, I knew again that God was really there too.

—PATRICIA HOUCK SPRINKLE

PRAY: *Even when my prayers seem unanswered, even when I see no sign of Your presence, I know You are with me, God, and I thank You.*

DO: Send this devotional to a friend who's discouraged by unanswered prayer.

WHEN YOUR PROBLEMS LOOK LARGER THAN LIFE

READ: *Now what I am commanding you today is not too difficult for you or beyond your reach.*

—DEUTERONOMY 30:11 (NIV)

REFLECT: Grandma and I had just settled down to visit when a piercing scream sent me running outside. "A dragon!" Three-year-old Rebecca hurled herself into my arms. "A dragon chased me!"

"Dragons are make-believe," I scolded.

"But I saw one!" Rebecca insisted. "He stuck out his tongue at me! He's hiding over there!" She pointed to a massive honeysuckle.

I looked. A four-inch green and gold gecko flicked its tongue, and I grabbed it. "Honey, it's only a lizard," I explained.

After much persuasion, she gingerly touched its back. "It looks like the dragons in my fairy tale book," she said.

So it did. The lizard was the same size as the picture of a dragon in her book.

Like Rebecca's "dragon," when my own problems seem larger than life, I turn to God, Who frees me from disabling fear and helps me reduce problems to a realistic, manageable size.

—PENNEY SCHWAB

PRAY: *Thank You, Father, for trusting me with problems I think are too big for me. I pray You are glorified in them.*

DO: Use this illustration to put a problem in perspective for a child or adult friend.

WHEN YOUR SECURITY IS IN SOMETHING OTHER THAN GOD

READ: *Even to your old age, I am He, And even to gray hairs I will carry you! I have made, and I will bear; Even I will carry, and will deliver you.*

—ISAIAH 46:4

REFLECT: When I was a child, my brother and father and I climbed a mountain in Colorado. I scampered up with them, without the least hesitation. But the trip down scared me to death. On one gravelly ledge, I lost my footing and started to slide toward a sharp drop-off. I was able to grab hold of a small tree, but there I was, feet dangling over what seemed to be a huge abyss. First I screamed and then I froze in absolute terror. Within minutes, I heard a strong voice calling to me from below. "Let go," said my dad. "Just let go!" He had hurried down ahead and was holding out his arms to me. I'll never forget that moment of having to make myself let go, knowing I'd have to fall in order to be safe. My father's arms never felt so good!

Is there some area of your life that needs to be released to God?"

—MARILYN MORGAN KING

PRAY: *You are my security, Father. Take away anything I'm clinging to other than You.*

DO: Tuck a picture of a cliff into your Bible to remind you to let go of your lifelines and let God catch you.

WHEN YOUR SECURITY
IS SHAKEN

◄○►

READ: *For I am the Lord, I do not change. . . .*

—MALACHI 3:6

REFLECT: The sound of burning timbers roused a Midwest farm family one winter night. They looked out the windows and saw the barn engulfed in flames.

Dashing outside in his pajamas, a ten-year-old boy entered the barn with only one thing on his mind—saving his palomino pony Buster. Amid falling debris, the youngster emerged seconds later with the animal, but the boy's success was short-lived. Outside, the noise and smoke and flames were even more terrifying to the pony than they had been in the barn. He reared free from the boy's hold and galloped back into the burning structure. In the morning, they found Buster dead in his familiar stall where he had thought he'd be safe.

Tragically, the pony made the same mistake many people do: thinking that security is a particular person, place or thing.

—FRED BAUER

PRAY: *Father, I know better than to try to find security in things other than You. Forgive me, Lord, for the many times I do that. Be my security today and always.*

DO: Give up the things you're seeking to find security in and turn to the Lord. He never changes.

WHEN YOUR SPIRITUAL ROOTS ARE SHALLOW

◄○►

READ: *Rooted and built up in Him and established in the faith, as you have been taught, abounding in it with thanksgiving.*

—COLOSSIANS 2:7

REFLECT: I was admiring the beautiful hardwood pews that a carpenter friend builds for places of worship. He personally selects the trees from which the pews are made. "I have to travel by plane halfway across the continent to where the trees grow. Then I hike for days through hardwood forests on the stormy side of the slopes."

"Why the stormy side?" I asked.

"That's where trees develop deep roots and firm cell structures because they must grow strong enough to withstand the prevailing winds. The trees on the sheltered side of the slopes have shallow roots and a coarse grain."

The prevailing winds that year were blowing rather fiercely on my side of the slope with family decisions to make and upheavals in my work schedule.

I found myself praying—really praying—for the courage to meet problems head-on, for the grace to confront difficult situations.

At the end of the year, I had gone a whole lot deeper with God.

—ALMA BARKMAN

PRAY: *Father, cause my life to have roots deep in You and a beautiful, smooth grain.*

DO: Pray for someone living on the stormy side of the slopes today.

WHEN YOUR TROUBLES
SEEM HERE TO STAY

—◇—

READ: *It came to pass....*

REFLECT: Although Uncle Jake, who did yard work for me, was an uneducated man by our standards, his scriptural knowledge was amazing. On one occasion he and I were working in my yard. As usual, Uncle Jake was whistling softly as he worked—a gospel hymn. At a pause I asked him what he considered his favorite Bible passage.

He leaned on his spading fork, pushed his sweat-stained hat back and scratched his chin. "Well, sir. I've lots of favorites, but there's one that has helped me most. It's found all through the Good Book, but it's just five ordinary words: 'and it came to pass.'"

I looked puzzled, so he continued. "Don't you see? I've known a heap of troubles, but they came to pass. They didn't come to stay."

—CHARLES M. DAVIS

PRAY: *Thank You, Lord, that my financial troubles came to pass; this sickness came to pass; worries about my kids came to pass.*

DO: Fill in the blank with your troubles: _____ came to pass; _____ came to pass; _____ came to pass.